VOLUME 73
NUMBER 11
NOVEMBER 2012

Current Biography ®

Cover: AFP/Getty Images

ISSN: 0011-3344
ISBN: 978-0-8242-1248-3
     978-0-8242-1143-1

RE
CT
/0(
C8
V. 7
No. /
2o1

A Note to Our Readers

Current Biography, which is published every month except December, presents articles on people who are prominent in the news—in popular culture, sports, science and technology, national and international affairs, business, and the visual and performing arts. The profiles in this periodical are objective rather than authorized, and the sources of information are newspapers, magazines, books, the Internet, and, in some cases, the biographees themselves. Each subject's preferred or professional name form is given in the heading of the article, with the full name supplied in the article itself. The heading of each profile includes the pronunciation of the name if it is unusual, date of birth if it is obtainable, and occupation. The article is supplemented by a list of selected references.

At the end of the year, all profiles published in the monthly issues will be cumulated alphabetically and printed in a single volume, *Current Biography Yearbook 2012.* These profiles will also be available on the electronic version of the publication, *Current Biography, 1940–Present.* Also available, in print and electronic form, are the profiles in *Current Biography International Yearbook.*

1. Marguerite Abouet

Born: 1971
Occupation: Graphic novelist

Born in the West African nation of Ivory Coast, Marguerite Abouet has been living in France since the age of twelve and currently lives near Paris with her husband and son. In her early thirties, she began work on a graphic novel about the everyday issues and concerns of a group of friends, young adults living in an Ivory Coast city in the late 1970s. The graphic novel, simply titled *Aya*, was published in France in 2005 and has sold more than 200,000 copies. In 2007, it was published in English in North America. Subsequent English translations of sequels followed: *Aya of Yop City* (2008), *Aya: The Secrets Come Out* (2009), *Aya: Life in Yop City* (2012), and *Aya: Love in Yop City* (2012).

AFP/Getty Images

In a review of *Aya of Yop City* for the *Wall Street Journal* (5 Sep. 2008), Davide Berretta observed that the book "aims to show a new side of Africa." That observation is equally valid for all five parts of the *Aya* series. Abouet was well aware that the news coverage of Africa—particularly in Europe and the United States—often focused on AIDS, famine, and civil wars; although she has not denied that those are serious problems, Abouet wanted to make the case that there is much more to Africa—something universal, such as adults and adolescents dealing with love, romance, friendship, and financial concerns. *Aya* has been translated into more than a dozen languages. Abouet, who wrote and outlined *Aya*, collaborated with her husband, Clément Oubrerie, an artist who illustrated the graphic novel. An animated film version of *Aya*, written and codirected by Abouet, is scheduled to be released in 2013.

EARLY LIFE IN ABIDJAN

Abouet was born in 1971 in Abidjan, Ivory Coast. Her childhood in Ivory Coast and her subsequent visits to her home country in later years provided the foundation for the descriptions and characters that populate *Aya*. By the time Abouet was born, Ivory Coast had achieved its independence from France; it had been a French colony until 1960. In an interview with Angela Ajayi for the online magazine *Wild River Review* (July 2012), Abouet offered a summary of the cultural and economic movements that followed the Ivory Coast's independence from France. She describes the new middle class of young, educated people who moved to Abidjan." Helped along by the economy of the time, all these new graduates found jobs. For relaxation, they formed clubs where they met after work or on weekends. That is also where they socialized and married. Their parents no longer had great influence on their life choices; they had been surpassed by the changes in the country and by this new freedom brought about by the 'Ivorian miracle.'" Abouet goes on to say that middle class women in Abidjan at this time enjoyed a newfound liberation. "They no longer yielded to their parents' authority in choosing a husband. Their level of education made them aware of their rights: the right to divorce, access to the pill, opportunities for professional careers." In fact, Abouet's parents were both products of this middle class.

AN AVID READER MOVES TO FRANCE

From a young age, Abouet loved stories, and she became an avid reader. However, one of her earliest influences, she told an interviewer for *The Brown Bookshelf* blog (31 Jan. 2010), was her grandfather. "I have always treasured the stories that my maternal grandfather told me around the fire during the holidays in the village," she said. "All of those stories in our oral tradition were rich, imaginative accounts of mythology, wonderful tales. He taught me to pay attention to what occurred around me, to listen to the stories, and then become a storyteller. These stories of the Ivory Coast provided fertile ground for my imagination."

When Abouet was twelve years old, she and her older brother were sent by their parents to Paris, France, where they lived with their great-uncle and pursued educations. Even though Abouet was in a new culture and a new country; she was familiar with the language because even after independence, French remained the official language of the Ivory Coast (although there are many dialects spoken in the country). In France she loved going to the library, reading the works of a variety of authors, such as William Shakespeare, science-fiction writer Jules Verne, and mystery writers such as Agatha Christie and Sir Arthur Conan Doyle.

TELLING HER STORIES, HER WAY

Despite living in France, far away from her place of birth, Abouet did not forget her home country and her upbringing. In fact, the idea to write about both had long been brewing inside her. Her idea was not only about the characters and stories, she told Ajayi, but also about fixing what she believed was a one-sided view of Africa in the mainstream Western media: "I had always felt the need to recollect my youth down there, the silliness I got into, the unbelievable stories about the quartier [the quarter], the families, the neighbors. I did not want to forget that part of my life, to hold on to those memories, and the desire to recount them got stronger with age. I felt a little guilty for being content in another country, far away from my family; in addition, I got so annoyed at the way in which the media systematically showed the bad side of the African continent, habitual litanies of wars, famine, of the 'sida,' and other disasters, that I wished to show the other side, to tell about daily modern life that also exists in Africa."

Prior to gaining success with the *Aya* series, Abouet worked as a legal assistant in Paris. She also wrote and tried to publish novels for young adults. However, as she has revealed in various interviews, she had a hard time getting those novels published—and ultimately gave up trying—because the publishers wanted to edit her books in a way that stripped them of all frank discussions of topics like sex and other mature themes.

GETTING STARTED AS A GRAPHIC NOVELIST

Abouet did not set out to become a graphic novelist. In fact, her introduction to that world came through comics, about which she had mixed feelings. "I feel like girls were not really involved in comics, and comics were not really for girls," Abouet told John Zuarino for *Bookslut* (May 2007). "I hated when I was young to read [stories of] superheroes. Except for Spider-Man. He was a normal guy—he was having affairs with girls. He had complicated stories with girls and his aunt and everything, so I felt he was closer to me. And he was beautiful also. I was in love with Spider-Man. But otherwise I didn't feel close to the superheroes. I wasn't concerned with them."

Marjane Satrapi, the author of the autobiographical graphic novel *Persepolis: The Story of a Childhood* (2002), which is about growing up in Iran, became a big influence on Abouet, inspiring her to write her graphic novel about a girl living in Abidjan, Ivory Coast, in the late 1970s. Abouet wanted to tell a real story about the adolescents and adults living in a city that at one point was her home. She based many of the characters on people she used to know, but the situations and events, albeit realistic, were fictionalized. In addition to relying on her memories of her upbringing in Ivory Coast, Abouet used the memories and experiences of her recent trips to Abidjan to provide her with inspiration.

Abouet has admitted many times that she cannot draw. On the other hand, her husband, Oubrerie, is an artist, so she asked him to illustrate her graphic novel. Abouet wrote the story and made storyboards, then she and her husband worked on the story together. Once the plot and storyboards were complete, Oubrerie began to work on the color illustrations. Not only was Oubrerie familiar with the story of Abouet's upbringing, but he had also traveled to the Ivory Coast many times.

AYA

The graphic novel the couple produced, *Aya*, was a big success in France, where it was first published in 2005 before being published in English in North America by Drawn & Quarterly, in 2007. The book would ultimately be translated into more than a dozen languages and win the 2006 Angouleme International Comics Festival prize for "first album."

Aya is about the title character, a nineteen-year-old girl, and her friends Adjoua and Bintou, as well as their families and friends. It is a lively, lighthearted, real, humorous tale of life in the Yopougon neighborhood during Ivory Coast's so-called Ivorian miracle, which was a relatively prosperous time for the West African nation. In a review for *Library Journal* (9 Jan. 2007), Melissa Aho called the book a "fun and charming story of a bygone era." Aho then concluded: "Mature themes and issues will appeal to adult audiences, but the unique Ivory Coast setting and the female central characters make this book ideal for harder-to-please older teenage girls." The stories and problems into which Abouet delves in the graphic novel are universal. Many young people can relate to stories of drinking and dancing, the desire to find companionship with a special someone, and the confusion and heartache that can come with romance—especially when it goes wrong. There are other problems, too. For example, Aya wants to study to become a doctor, whereas her father is more concerned with her finding a good husband and marrying well.

> "I got so annoyed at the way in which the media systematically showed the bad side of the African continent . . . that I wished to show the other side, to tell about daily modern life that also exists in Africa."

Although Aya is certainly part of the story, much of the time she is simply the witness and observer. Toward the end of the book, Aya's friend Adjoua gives birth to a baby boy (the pregnancy was not planned). Adjoua says the father is a young man named Moussa, who is the son of a wealthy local man named Bonaventure Sissoko. The claim is suspicious, which becomes apparent in the sequel.

THE *AYA* SERIES

The sequel, *Aya of Yop City*, picks up where *Aya* leaves off. In the first few pages of the book, Bonaventure Sissoko is standing over the baby and asks Adjoua, her father, and others gathered around, "Tell me the truth, when you see this baby, does he look like my son Moussa?" While Adjoua's father tries pitifully to explain, Bonaventure does not buy the explanations. The answer is obviously no. In fact, it later becomes apparent that the baby looks like Mamadou, a local playboy. Mamadou may be good-looking and charming, but Adjoua cannot depend on him for support. Mamadou is not the only undependable man in the story. Aya's friend Bintou falls for Gregoire, who claims to be successful.

The overlapping stories of Yop City would have little impact in a graphic novel without the proper illustration style, one that captures the mood, language, and culture of the time. In a review for the website *ComicMix* (27 Oct. 2008), Andrew Wheeler focuses on the drawings: "As in the first book, Oubrerie's loose, vibrant art captures the feel of Ivory Coast—his sunlight has an almost physical quality and his line delights in the possibilities of the many bold patterns worn by the women of Yop City. His character's expressions can sometimes feel a bit flat—he draws them without eyelids, so eyes are always wide open, with only size and shape to define emotion—but their body language makes up for that." At the time of Wheeler's review, four graphic novels in the *Aya* series had been published in France, where they had sold more than 200,000 copies. Furthermore, because of Abouet's efforts, her French publisher, Édition Gallimard, sold inexpensive, softcover copies of the *Aya* series in the Ivory Coast.

In *Aya: The Secrets Come Out*, published in English in 2009, Abouet continues telling the stories of the everyday lives of the young people of Yop City. In a review for *Library Journal* (7 Jan. 2010), Martha Cornog wrote: "With much of the story focusing on a Miss Yop City beauty pageant, the level-headed Aya helps family and friends with their problems while allowing them to find their own way. *Aya*'s setting and detail conjure the appeal of a different place and time, whereas the characters resonate in the universality of their hopes." Abouet continued to tell the delightfully funny and touching story of Aya and her friends, family, and neighbors in *Aya: Life in Yop City* and *Aya: Love in Yop City*. The latter contains the last three chapters of the *Aya* series, in which are mature themes: For example, Aya must deal with a shady professor who has taken advantage of her. However, the volume, unlike all previous *Aya* editions, contains additional material, such as an afterword from Abouet, as well as recipes, sketches, and a guide to the slang of the Ivory Coast.

SUGGESTED READING

Abouet, Marguerite. "Drawing on the Universal in Africa: An Interview with Marguerite Abouet." Interview by Angela Ajayi. *Wild River Review.* Wild River Review, July 2012. Web. 21 Aug. 2012.

Aho, Melissa. "*Aya.*" Review of *Aya*, by Marguerite Abouet and Clement Oubrerie. *Library Journal.* Library Journal, 15 Jan. 2007. Web. 21 Aug. 2012.

Berretta, Davide. "The Cartoon Heart of Africa." *Wall Street Journal.* Dow Jones, 5 Sep. 2008. Web. 23 Aug. 2012.

Cornog, Martha. "From *Aya* to *Zapt!*: Twenty-Four Graphic Novels for African American History Month." Review of *Aya*, by Marguerite Abouet and Clement Oubrerie. *Library Journal.* Library Journal, 7 Jan. 2010. Web. 21 Aug. 2012.

Wheeler, Andrew. "Review: *Aya of Yop City* by Marguerite Abouet and Clement Oubrerie." *ComicMix.* ComicMix, 27 Oct. 2008. Web. 21 Aug. 2012.

—*Dmitry Kiper*

Michael Chabon

Born: May 24, 1963
Occupation: Writer

"[Michael] Chabon is more or less incapable of writing a boring sentence," Steve Almond wrote for the *Los Angeles Times* (4 Oct. 2009). That sentiment is frequently echoed by others; Chabon, who won a Pulitzer Prize for *The Amazing Adventures of*

Getty Images

Kavalier & Clay (2000), about a pair of cousins who strike it big during the golden age of comic books, has been called one of the most gifted writers of his generation. Michael Hayward wrote for the quarterly Canadian magazine *Geist* that Chabon's "genre-defying success with *The Amazing Adventures of Kavalier & Clay* . . . and *The Yiddish Policemen's Union* demonstrate that 'popular success' and 'critical success' need not be mutually exclusive categories." Commenting on an additional dichotomy, a reviewer for the *St. Paul Pioneer Press* (17 May 2007) marveled, "He may be the only novelist in history to write for both the *New York Review of Books*, where he recently had a ravishing essay on Cormac McCarthy and apocalypse fiction, and *Details*, where his latest contribution concerned 'the man purse.'" Chabon explained his wide-ranging sensibilities to Charles Matthews for the *San Jose Mercury News* (11 Nov. 2007): "I hate to see great works of literature ghettoized, whereas others that conform to the rules, conventions, and procedures of the genre we call literary fiction get accorded greater esteem and privilege. To me, it's about pleasure, and the pleasure of reading, and I like to define pleasure broadly."

EARLY YEARS

Chabon (pronounced SHAY-bon) was born on May 24, 1963, in Washington, DC. His father, Robert Chabon, was a medical student who went on to become a noted pediatrician. His mother, Sharon (née Cohen), was a homemaker. Chabon's father also earned a law degree, and later in life was a litigator in cases related to medicine and health care. The family moved frequently during Chabon's early years, living in Pennsylvania, New York, and Arizona, among other places. When he was five years old, his younger brother, Stephen, was born. Chabon wrote in *Manhood for Amateurs* (2009), his book of personal essays, "I had learned to work a record player, tell lies, read the funny pages, and feel awkward at parties. But it was not until that morning, in early September 1968, that my story truly began. Until my brother was born, I had no one to tell it to."

The following year the family settled in Columbia, Maryland, a planned community established in 1967 and designed to be racially and economically integrated. Chabon has said that watching the town grow had a profound effect on his future career. "It was this incredibly powerful demonstration of what an imagination could accomplish in the real world," he told Stephen Kiehl for the *Baltimore Sun* (May 13, 2007). "It was like an act of magic. It was like somebody saying abracadabra. And here, in this place where there was nothing, there is now a house and a shopping center and a pool." He continued, "It made this powerful, magical impression on me that you could say you were going to do something and, in a way, all you needed to do was name it. . . . By naming streets, by naming villages, by naming neighborhoods . . . by doing that, you could cause things to come into existence." Chabon occupied himself by wandering the town's vacant lots and playgrounds, playing in the neighbors' yards, and riding his bicycle. He was also an avid baseball fan.

In 1975, Chabon's parents divorced. Chabon's father moved to Pennsylvania to become the chief of pediatrics at a Pittsburgh hospital. Michael and his brother spent summers and holidays with their father and new stepmother, Shelley, a speech pathologist. The city of Pittsburgh, like the town of Columbia, became immensely important to Chabon, and is featured in much of writing.

Following her divorce, Chabon's mother enrolled at the University of Baltimore, earning a law degree when Michael and Stephen were ages fourteen and nine, respectively. When she took a new job at a federal agency that required a long commute, Chabon took over many of the household tasks, including cooking.

As a teenager, Chabon was socially awkward and semi-reclusive, holing up in his room to listen to music and read. He was particularly fond of science fiction novels and comic books, and still often describes himself to interviewers as a "geek." "My secret confederates were the works of Monty Python, H. P. Lovecraft, the cartoonist Vaughan Bodé, and the Ramones, among many others; they kept me watered and fed," he wrote in an op-ed piece for the *New York Times* (13 Apr. 2004). "It was not long before I began to write: stories, poems, snatches of autobiographical jazz. . . . But the main reason I wrote stories—and the reason that I keep on writing them today—was not to express myself. I started to write because once it had been nourished, stoked, and liberated by those secret confederates, I could not hold back the force of my imagination. I had been freed."

EDUCATION

After a brief stint at Carnegie-Mellon University, Chabon entered the University of Pittsburgh, where he edited the student literary magazine for a year and read such authors as William Faulkner and Jorge Luis Borges for the first time. In 1984, he earned a bachelor's degree in literature. He then entered the MFA program at the University of California, Irvine. As his master's thesis, he turned in a coming-of-age novel he titled *The Mysteries of Pittsburgh*. Chabon's professor, Donald Heiney (himself a novelist who wrote under the pen name MacDonald Harris), was so impressed by the manuscript that he sent it off to an agent without informing Chabon. A bidding war ensued among publishers, and Chabon ultimately earned a six-figure advance, a noteworthy accomplishment for a young, unknown author. "I'm kind of a poster boy for the more tangible benefits that a good writing program can bestow," he quipped in an essay included in *Manhood for Amateurs*.

THE LAUNCH OF A LITERARY CAREER

The Mysteries of Pittsburgh was published in 1988. The book takes place during the summer after its protagonist, Art Bechstein, has graduated from the University of

Pittsburgh. The son of a mafia money launderer, Art wants only to enjoy a last summer of adventure before embarking on adult life and a career as a stockbroker. He soon becomes romantically involved with both Arthur Lecomte, a charismatic gay man, and Phlox Lombardi, a shy and somewhat odd young woman.

Because the novel was widely assumed to be semi-autobiographical, conjecture about Chabon's sexuality raged in literary circles. He was included by the editors of *Newsweek* in a feature on up-and-coming gay writers and felt compelled to issue a public denial. He asserted, however, that he was not upset about the mistake, because it had introduced his work to a whole new group of fans. Chabon later confirmed that he had once been engaged for a time in a same-sex relationship, and he employed gay characters and themes in several of his later works.

Amid the media interest in the amount of his advance and his sexual predilections, *The Mysteries of Pittsburgh* generated excitement in the book world. Alice McDermott's review for the *New York Times* (3 Apr. 1988), for example, was measured but still greatly enthusiastic. She wrote, "Here is a first novel by a talented young writer that is full of all the delights, and not a few of the disappointments, inherent in any early work of serious fiction. There is the pleasure of a fresh voice and a keen eye, of watching a writer clearly in love with language and literature, youth and wit, expound and embellish upon the world as he sees it, balanced by a scarcity of well-developed characters. . . . [Chabon] has learned well from the writers he appears to admire—F. Scott Fitzgerald especially—and his control over his story, the wonderful use he makes of each description, of Pittsburgh itself, are often astonishing." She concluded, "[T]here is much to admire here, and what the novel lacks in insight it compensates for in language, wit, and ambition, in the sheer exuberance of its voice: the voice of a young writer with tremendous skill as he discovers, joyously, just what his words can do."

> *"The pure reach and music and weight of Chabon's imagination are extraordinary, born of brilliant ambition you don't even notice because it is so deeply entertaining."*

In the wake of the publicity, Chabon—who declined both an offer to model jeans for a Gap ad campaign and a chance to be on *People* magazine's "Fifty Most Beautiful" list—remained characteristically modest. "I was one of the last first-novelists to get in that period when New York publishing was looking for the next hot thing," he told Sam Whiting for the *San Francisco Chronicle* (31 Mar. 1999). In 2008, *The Mysteries of Pittsburgh* was made into a film featuring Nick Nolte as the mobster father, and a young actor named Jon Foster as Art.

SOPHOMORE NOVEL

In 1990, Chabon published a short-story collection, *A Model World and Other Stories*, that was well received. He struggled for years with his next novel, which had as its main character an architect endeavoring to construct the ideal baseball park. After writing more than 1,000 words, he abandoned the effort in 1992. (An annotated fragment of the unfinished book, which had the working title *Fountain City*, was published in the literary magazine *McSweeney's* in December 2010.) Within a few months of turning his focus from *Fountain City*, Chabon completed *Wonder Boys*. Published in 1995, the novel follows the travails of Grady Tripp, a middle-aged writing instructor and novelist who had once been considered one of the most exceptional literary talents of his generation. Grady, who lives and works in Pittsburgh, now spends his days conducting an extramarital affair with his college's female chancellor (whose husband chairs the school's English Department) and drinking to excess. He is thus unable to complete a long-awaited magnum opus and must convince his flamboyantly gay editor that the manuscript is almost ready for publication. Over the course of the novel, Grady and one of his students, James, become embroiled in a series of comical criminal adventures. The character of Grady is based on Chuck Kinder, a University of Pittsburgh professor.

Most reviewers felt that Chabon, despite the lengthy period between novels, had avoided the sophomore slump. "Mr. Chabon is that rare thing, an intelligent lyrical writer," Robert Ward wrote for the *New York Times Book Review* (9 Apr. 1995, online). "Because his comedy always reins in his romantic impulses, his work seems to reflect a nature that is at once passionate and satirical. The result is a tone of graceful melancholy punctuated by a gentle and humane good humor." In 2000, *Wonder Boys* became a feature film starring Michael Douglas as Grady, and Tobey Maguire as James.

THE AMAZING ADVENTURES OF KAVALIER & CLAY

Chabon published another collection of short stories in 1999. The collection, *Werewolves in Their Youth*, was credited in part to August Van Zorn, a fictitious pulp writer who had appeared briefly in *Wonder Boys*. In 2000, Chabon published *The Amazing Adventures of Kavalier & Clay*. The Pulitzer Prize–winning novel traces the lives of two cousins: Josef Kavalier, who has come to New York City after escaping Nazi-occupied Prague, and Sammy Klayman, the son of a vaudeville strongman named the Mighty Molecule. It's the golden age of comic book publishing, and together the two develop such popular titles as *The Escapist*, *The Monitor*, and *Luna Moth*. *The Amazing Adventures of Kavalier & Clay* was based, in part, on Joe Shuster and Jerry Siegel, the creators of Superman, who had sold the rights to their character to DC Comics for a few hundred dollars in the late 1930s. *The Escapist* storylines described in the novel were later adapted as comic stories and released in three graphic novels.

In addition to winning the Pulitzer, *The Amazing Adventures of Kavalier & Clay* met with near-unanimous critical acclaim. In a representative review, Donna Seaman wrote for *Booklist* (Aug. 2000), "Virtuoso Chabon takes intense delight in the practice of his art, and never has his joy been more palpable than in this funny and profound tale of exile, love, and magic." In the flurry of interviews that followed his Pulitzer win, Chabon explained to journalists how important comics had been to him as a child, particularly after he discovered the iconic work of Jack Kirby at Marvel. "These characters were more screwed up, had neuroses, problems," he told Lewis Buzzbee for the *New York Times* (24 Sep. 2000). "The idea that it would be lonely to be a superhero. It makes it easier to identify with—wow, Spider-Man is lonely, too." Additionally, comic books provided a connection to his father, who was also a fan, and the two often browsed comic shops together.

THE YIDDISH POLICEMAN'S UNION

In 2007, Chabon published *The Yiddish Policeman's Union*, a hard-boiled detective story set in Sitka, Alaska. A work of alternative history, the book takes as its premise that the Jews of Eastern Europe, displaced by World War II, have been allowed to settle in a remote corner of Alaska. (Chabon drew upon the little-known fact that Franklin Roosevelt's secretary of the interior had once proposed a similar plan.) In the fictional enclave, alcoholic police detective Meyer Landsman and his sidekick, Berko Shemets, must solve a mystery involving a murder, a mafia-like group called the Verbovers, and a Zionist geopolitical plot.

Writing a book featuring Jewish criminals and pidgin Yiddish left Chabon, who is Jewish, open to charges of being a self-hating anti-Semite. "Its satire has the effect, intended or not, of treating Israel as something simultaneously fanatical and ridiculous," Samuel Freedman wrote for the *Jewish Exponent* (26 Jul. 2007). "One of the running gags of the novel is the absurdity of shtetl life transplanted into Alaska. The unspoken inference is that it is just as unnatural for Jews to have plopped themselves down in a Middle Eastern desert. And when Chabon refers to the Sitka Jews having pushed out the indigenous Tlingit Indians, his metaphor needs no footnote to be understood." Despite such criticism, most reviewers were dazzled. Terrence Rafferty, writing for the *New York Times* (13 May 2007), called it a "funny, humane, wised-up novel," and in the *Washington Post* (13 May 2007), Elizabeth McCracken enthused, "Reading *The Yiddish Policemen's Union* is like watching a gifted athlete invent a sport using elements of every other sport there is—balls, bats, poles, wickets, javelins and saxophones." McCracken continued, "The pure reach and music and weight of Chabon's imagination are extraordinary, born of brilliant ambition you don't even notice because it is so deeply entertaining. He invents every corner of this strange world—the slang of the 'Sitkaniks,' their history, discount houses, divey bars, pie shops. Despite the complications of the plot, the details of the world are every bit as enthralling."

Chabon published *Telegraph Avenue* in 2012. The plot of the novel revolves around the intertwined lives of two families, one black and one white, who co-own a used-record store on the iconic street in Oakland, California. The actual Telegraph Avenue that inspired the book extends almost five miles, from the downtown section of Oakland to the campus of the University of California, Berkeley. The street's nature changes every few blocks—with some sections lined with public housing and others filled with trendy clothing shops and unique bookstores. "I guess that for a guy who likes hanging around the borderlands—between genres, cultures, musics, legacies, styles—the appeal of Telegraph lies in the way it reflects a local determination to find your path irrespective of boundary lines, picking up what you can, shaking off what you can, along the way," Chabon wrote for the *Atlantic* (10 Jan. 2011).

OTHER WORKS

Chabon is also the author of *Summerland* (2002), a baseball-themed fantasy novel for young adults, and *The Astonishing Secret of Awesome Man* (2011), a picture book for children. His other books include the short Sherlock Holmes pastiche *The Final Solution: A Story of Detection* (2004); the novel *Gentlemen of the Road: A Tale of Adventure* (2007), which had been originally published in serial form in the *New York Times Magazine*; and the essay collection *Maps and Legends: Reading and Writing along the Borderlands* (2008). He has contributed to the occasional screenplay, including those for *Spider-Man 2* (2004) and *John Carter* (2012).

PERSONAL LIFE

In 1987, Chabon married the poet Iola "Lollie" Groth. He wrote in *Manhood for Amateurs* that the marriage had been, "in a way that I found almost intoxicating—the way slamming a trunk lid on your hand or missing a step as you climb a stairway in the dark can be intoxicating—a great mistake." The couple divorced in 1990. Two years later, Chabon met Ayelet Waldman, an Israeli-born attorney, on a blind date. They married in 1993. In addition to writing poetry, Waldman is also an essayist and mystery writer. She and Chabon have four children—Sophie, Zeke, Rosie, and Abe.

In 2010, Chabon, who lives with his family in Berkeley, was elected chairman of the MacDowell Colony, the oldest artists' colony in the United States. In 2012, he was inducted into the Academy of American Letters. Chabon was also featured on a 2006 episode of *The Simpsons* along with writers Tom Wolfe, Gore Vidal, and Jonathan Franzen.

SUGGESTED READING

Almond, Steve. "Manhood Bound." *Los Angeles Times* 4 Oct. 2009: E12. Print.

Chabon, Michael. *Manhood for Amateurs*. New York: HarperCollins, 2009. Print.

---. "That's Why I Came" *Atlantic*. Atlantic Monthly Group, 10 Jan. 2011. Web. 5 June 2012.

Cohen, Patricia. "The Frozen Chosen." *New York Times* 29 Apr. 2007: B1. Print.

Freedman, Samuel. "Chabon's Choice." *Jewish Exponent* 26 July 2007: 25. Print.

Kiehl, Stephen. "NovelBuilder." *Baltimore Sun*. 13 May 2007: E1. Print.

Kirschling, Gregory. "The New Adventures of Michael Chabon." *EW.com*. Entertainment Weekly, 9 May 2007. Web. 6 June 2012.

Whiting, Sam. "Writer's 'Wonder Year.'" *San Francisco Chronicle*. 31 Mar. 1999: E1. Print.

—Mari Rich

Pavel Datsyuk

Born: July 20, 1978
Occupation: Hockey player

Since his National Hockey League (NHL) debut in 2001, Pavel Datsyuk has developed a reputation as a skilled offensive player, with his remarkable hand-eye coordination, his deceptive speed, and his stick-handling ability. He is consistent, scoring twenty or more goals in seven consecutive seasons (2003 to 2010). However, Datsyuk has not only garnered attention for his offensive abilities; he is also widely regarded for his defensive play. "If you're down a goal in the last minute, who do you want out there—[Alexander] Ovechkin, [Sidney] Crosby, [Evgeni] Malkin or Datsyuk? Any of them," said Detroit Red Wings coach Mike Babcock to Mitch Albom for the *Detroit Free Press* (19 Apr. 2009). "But if you're up a goal in the last minute and need to protect the lead, who would you want? You'd want Pav." Over three consecutive seasons (2008 to 2010) Datsyuk was the recipient of the Frank J. Selke Trophy, which recognizes the league's best defensive forward. In the 2007 and 2008 season he led the NHL in takeaways, with 144, a league record. During eleven years in Detroit, Datsyuk has helped lead his team to two Stanley Cup titles.

NHLI via Getty Images

EARLY LIFE

Pavel Valerievich Datsyuk was born on July 20, 1978, in Ekaterinburg (formerly known as Sverdlovsk), the fourth-largest city in Russia and one of the country's industrial and economic hubs. His father, Valery, worked as a van driver, and his mother, Galina, was a cook for a military post. Datsyuk lived with his parents and older sister in a cramped, three-room apartment. The building also overlooked a makeshift ice skating rink, where he first learned to play hockey.

Datsyuk honed his skills at the Yunost Sports Academy, in Ekaterinburg, and trained under the watchful eye of Valeri Goloukhov. Growing up, Datsyuk also played for the local youth hockey team Yunost Ekaterinburg. However, he almost gave up the sport, following the untimely death of his mother, who passed away from cancer when he was sixteen years old—an event that affected him deeply. "I felt guilty," he told Albom. "I didn't know she was so sick. I thought she would get better. When I look back, I think she took that last vacation with me because she knew she was going to die." At first, a grieving Datsyuk struggled to cope with her death. "I lost myself," he admitted to Albom.

PROFESSIONAL HOCKEY IN RUSSIA

Despite his grief, Datsyuk eventually returned to the hockey rink. The eighteen-year-old center started the 1996 and 1997 season playing for SKA Yekaterinburg in the Pervaya Liga, a feeder league for the now-defunct Russian Superleague (RSL). In his position as center, Datsyuk's role is that of the playmaker, passing between the two wings to set up a goal.

Datsyuk scored two goals and had two assists in eighteen games for SKA Yekaterinburg before signing with Spartak Yekaterinburg, a team that competed in the RSL, which was not only the country's top professional ice hockey league but also ranked as the second-best league in the world, after the NHL. The Kontinental Hockey League (KHL), also regarded as the premier association in Europe, has since replaced the RSL.

In his 1996 and 1997 season with Spartak, Datsyuk appeared in thirty-six games, in which he had twelve goals and ten assists. He spent the 1997 and 1998 with Dynamo-Energiya Yekaterinburg, the farm club for HC Dynamo Moscow, a hockey team competing in the Western Conference of the KHL. After making twenty-four appearances and amassing three goals and five assists for the Dynamo squad, Datsyuk scored seven goals and had eight assists in twenty-two games for Dynamo-Energiya Yekaterinburg 2, the team's minor-league affiliate in the Pervaya Liga (also referred to as RUS-3).

NHL DRAFT PICK

During the 1997 and 1998 season, Datsyuk unexpectedly caught the attention of Hakan Andersson, the European director of scouting for the Detroit Red Wings of the NHL. "I travelled out to see [defensive prospect] Dmitri Kalinin play. His team was playing Datsyuk's team. Kalinin was an 18-year-old and Datsyuk in his last junior season," Andersson told Steve Simons for *Canoe.ca* (28 May 2008). "I went to see him one more time. I put him on the list. My main concern was he was small. I was afraid he would make the world junior team. That would have exposed him."

In June 1998 Datsyuk was the 171st player selected overall by the Detroit Red Wings, in the sixth round of the NHL Entry Draft. He had been previously passed over in the 1996 and 1997 NHL drafts, mainly over concerns about his size; at the time Datsyuk's height was five feet seven and he weighed about 150 pounds, which was considered undersized by league standards. After being drafted into the NHL, Datsyuk remained in Russia, where he continued to develop his skills. He began the 1998 and 1999 season with minor-league affiliate Dynamo-Energiya Yekaterinburg 2. After appearing in ten games and recording an equal number of goals and assists—fourteen—for the team, Datsyuk was subsequently assigned to Dynamo-Energiya Yekaterinburg, where he amassed twenty-one goals and twenty-three assists in thirty-five games to close out the season.

Datsyuk followed that up with a one-goal, three-assist performance for Dynamo-Energiya Yekaterinburg in 1999 and 2000. The next season he played for Ak Bars Kazan, a dominant club in the RSL. Despite suffering a leg injury, he still managed nine goals and seventeen assists in forty-two games. Datsyuk was also a member of the Russian team that competed at the 2001 International Ice Hockey Federation (IIHF) World Championship.

NHL DEBUT AND THE FIRST STANLEY CUP

In 2001 Datsyuk received an invitation to the Detroit Red Wings' training camp, where his impressive play quickly turned heads. "His first day of training camp he had the flu," former Red Wings teammate Steve Yzerman told Helene St. James in an interview that appeared in *USA Today* (20 Jan. 2009). "From the second day on, he wowed us." Datsyuk earned a spot on the club's 2001 and 2002 NHL roster, which also included veterans Brendan Shanahan, Niklas Lidstrom, and Chris Chelios; fellow Russians Igor Larionov and Sergei Fedorov; and newly signed free agents Brett Hull and Luc Robitaille.

During the eighty-two-game regular season, Datsyuk became a fixture in the Detroit Red Wings' starting lineup. He was part of an effective forward line with second-year player Boyd Devereaux and Hull, who dubbed the trio "Two Kids and an Old Goat." (The forward line, which consists of a left wing, a center, and a right wing, is responsible for most of the team's scoring.) Hull's veteran presence proved to be a benefit to the rookie Datsyuk, whose eleven goals and twenty-four assists in seventy games helped his team capture the Western Conference Central Division title as well as the NHL Presidents' Trophy.

After defeating the Vancouver Canucks and St. Louis Blues, the Red Wings advanced to the best-of-seven Western Conference championship, where they beat out the Colorado Avalanche and earned a berth to the Stanley Cup finals, another best-of-seven contest. The Carolina Hurricanes proved to be no match for the Red Wings, who won the series in five games. During his team's playoff run, Datsyuk appeared in twenty-one games, racking up three goals and three assists en route to his first Stanley Cup victory. That year he was part of the Western Conference squad that competed in the NHL YoungStars, an exhibition game among the league's top rookies that is held during the NHL All-Star weekend in January. He scored one of the team's thirteen goals en route to a six-run victory over their Eastern Conference counterparts.

PROMINENCE WITH THE RED WINGS

In his sophomore season (2002 and 2003), Datsyuk managed to notch twelve goals and thirty-nine assists despite being sidelined by a strained right knee injury that limited him to sixty-four regular-season games. He was again paired on the forward line with Hull; Henrik Zetterberg, a highly regarded rookie prospect from Sweden, replaced Devereaux. For the second straight season, the Detroit Red Wings won the Western Conference division and advanced to the Stanley Cup playoffs, where the upstart Mighty Ducks of Anaheim swept the defending champions in the first round. Datsyuk went scoreless in the four-game series.

In June 2003 Datsyuk signed a one-year $1.5 million contract, which included an option to remain with the Red Wings for the 2004 and 2005 season. In each of his first two seasons, he had earned less than a million dollars. Following the exodus of Sergei Fedorov, who had signed a five-year $40 million deal with the Ducks, Datsyuk was expected to play a larger role in the Red Wings' offense during the 2003 and 2004 season. For the last two seasons, Fedorov had been one of the team's scoring leaders, along with Hull and Shanahan.

In 2003 and 2004 Datsyuk received more ice time, averaging eighteen minutes and sixteen seconds per game, up from the fifteen minutes and twenty-eight seconds he averaged the previous season. With the increased playing time, he improved his offensive production, scoring a team-high thirty goals and thirty-eight assists in seventy-five games for the Red Wings, who won a league-best forty-eight games to clinch their third consecutive division title. After defeating the Nashville Predators four games to two in the first round of the Stanley Cup playoffs, Detroit was eliminated in the second round by the Calgary Flames. Datsyuk went scoreless with six assists in twelve playoff games. He also made his first NHL All-Star appearance as a reserve for the Western Conference team, who was defeated by the Eastern squad. Internationally, Datsyuk represented Russia at the 2003 IIHF World Championship and the 2004 World Cup of Hockey.

CORNERSTONE OF THE RED WINGS FRANCHISE

On September 15, 2004, the NHL collective bargaining agreement (CBA) expired, provoking a labor disagreement between league owners and the players association that resulted in the cancellation of the entire 2004 to 2005 season. In anticipation of the NHL lockout, Datsyuk agreed to terms with his former club HC Dynamo Moscow. During the 2004–2005 season, he scored fifteen goals and seventeen assists in forty-seven games, earning MVP honors while helping Dynamo Moscow claim the 2005 Russian Superleague Championship.

In July 2005 the owners and the players association reached a new CBA that set the league-wide salary cap at $39 million—more than half of what the Red Wings had previously spent. Despite the cap constraints, the Red Wings managed to sign Datsyuk, a restricted free agent, to a two-year, $7.8 million deal in late September. In 2005 and 2006 he recorded twenty-eight goals in seventy-five games. Datsyuk also ranked among the league's top ten in assists, with fifty-nine, for the Red Wings, who amassed a league-best fifty-eight victories to win the Presidents' Trophy. However, the team failed to advance past the first round of the 2006 Stanley Cup playoffs, losing to the Edmonton Oilers in six games; Datsyuk notched three assists in five of those games. Following the playoffs, Datsyuk, who had only logged twenty-two penalty minutes during the regular season,

"If you're up a goal in the last minute and need to protect the lead, who would you want? You'd want Pav."

was presented with the Lady Byng Memorial Trophy for sportsmanlike conduct. He also competed with the national team, winning his second bronze at the 2005 IIHF World Championship and finishing fourth at the 2006 Winter Olympics in Turin, Italy.

In 2006 and 2007 Datsyuk was a model of consistency and durability, putting up numbers similar to the previous season. His twenty-seven goals and sixty assists in seventy-nine games helped lead the Red Wings to another Western Conference division title. Less than a week before the playoffs, Datsyuk agreed to a seven-year contract extension worth nearly $47 million. His team improved on last season's playoff performance, advancing past the Calgary Flames and San Jose Sharks in the first and second rounds, respectively. However, the Red Wings were defeated in the Western Conference finals by the Ducks, the eventual Stanley Cup champions. During the team's playoff run, Datsyuk was the scoring leader, with eight goals; he also had eight assists. Datsyuk was also the recipient of the Lady Byng award for the second consecutive time.

SECOND STANLEY CUP

Datsyuk's breakthrough season came in 2007 and 2008. He recorded a personal best of thirty-one goals, as well as a team-high sixty-six assists, while appearing in all eighty-two regular-season games. Another individual accomplishment included his second All-Star selection. For the third straight season, the Red Wings captured the Central Division West; they were also winners of the Presidents' Trophy for the second time in three years.

Datsyuk and his teammates faced off against the Nashville Predators in the first-round playoff series, which the Red Wings won in six games. They proved dominant in the second round, sweeping the Colorado Avalanche in four to reach the Western Conference finals. Datsyuk had a memorable performance in game 3 of the series; he scored three goals against the Dallas Stars to record his first career hat trick. The Red Wings went on to eliminate the Stars in six games and advance to the 2008 Stanley Cup Finals, which they won four games to two against the Pittsburgh Penguins. In the championship series, Datsyuk notched a total of three assists in two of the team's victories: one in game 4 and two in the deciding game 6. His lone goal came during a triple overtime loss in game 5.

2008 TO 2010

Following the Stanley Cup playoffs, Datsyuk was honored with the Lady Byng Trophy for the third year in a row, becoming the first NHL player to achieve this feat in more than seventy years. He was also awarded the Frank J. Selke Trophy, which recognizes the best defensive forward in the league. Datsyuk garnered further recognition for being one of only two players to receive both the Lady Byng and Selke trophies during their careers.

Datsyuk's offensive numbers in 2008 and 2009 were nearly identical to those of the prior season. In eighty-one appearances, he amassed a career high of thirty-two goals as well as sixty-five assists, the second-most of his career. The Red Wings finished the season with fifty-one victories, the best record in the Central West and the second-best record in the Western Conference. After completing a four-game sweep of the Columbus Blue Jackets in the first round of the playoffs, the Red Wings advanced to the second round, where they defeated the Ducks in seven games. They dominated the Chicago Blackhawks in the Western Conference finals, winning four out of five games to earn their second straight berth in the finals of the Stanley Cup. In a rematch of last year's championship series, the Red Wings went head-to-head with the Penguins, who overcame a three games-to-two deficit to win the Stanley Cup. Datsyuk recorded one goal and eight assists in sixteen postseason games. His 2008 and 2009 honors included a fourth consecutive Lady Byng Trophy; a second straight Selke Trophy; and an ESPY nod for Best NHL Player Award.

Datsyuk continued to provide an offensive spark for the team during the 2009 and 2010 season, scoring twenty-seven goals and forty-three assists in eighty games. The Red Wings, winners of forty-four regular-season games, finished second in the Central division and fifth overall in the conference. Datsyuk not only led his team in goals scored, with twenty-seven, but he also had forty-three assists, which was the second-highest total, behind Zetterberg. After besting the Phoenix Coyotes in seven games during the first round of the playoffs, the Red Wings fell in five games to the San Jose Sharks in the second round. Datsyuk, the recipient of a third consecutive Selke Trophy, was voted to his third All-Star game but did not participate due to a hip injury. He also competed at the 2010 IIHF World Championship in Germany, where the Russian national team earned a second-place finish, behind the gold-medal winning Czech Republic squad. Datsyuk, who scored six goals and one assist over the course of the tournament, was named best forward.

2010 TO 2012

Despite an injury-plagued 2010 and 2011 season, Datsyuk still managed to record twenty goals and thirty-six assists in fifty-six games. His team regained the Central Division title, after playing forty-seven regular-season games. For the second straight season, the Red Wings met the Coyotes in the first round of the playoffs. However, this time they defeated the Coyotes in four straight games and went on to face the Sharks, in a rematch of the last season's second round. The Red Wings were unceremoniously eliminated from the Stanley Cup playoffs after losing to the Sharks in seven games.

In 2011 and 2012 Datsyuk remained one of his team's offensive leaders, recording nineteen goals and a team-leading forty-eight assists in seventy games for the Red Wings, who finished third in the Central and fifth in the conference. However, their postseason was short-lived; they failed to make it past the first round after being defeated in five games by the Nashville Predators. Datsyuk was nominated for the Selke Trophy, which was ultimately awarded to Patrice Bergeron of the Boston Bruins.

Datsyuk has established the PD13 Hockey School in his native city of Ekaterinburg—PD13 incorporates his initials and his jersey number. He lives in Detroit, Michigan, with his wife, Svetlana and their daughter, Elizabeth.

SUGGESTED READING

Cannella, Stephen. "The NHL." *Sports Illustrated*. Time Inc., 22 Dec. 2003. Web. 10 Aug. 2012. Cazeneuve, Brian. "Disgusting, but in A Good Way." *Sports Illustrated*. Time Inc., 2 May 2011. Web. 10 Aug. 2012.

Farber, Michael. "Staring down the End." *Sports Illustrated*. Time Inc., 15 Mar. 2010. Web. 10 Aug. 2012.

---. "The Third Russian." *Sports Illustrated*. Time Inc., 13 Apr. 2009. Web. 10 Aug. 2012.

Helka, Mike. "Datsyuk, Red Wings Destined for Each Other." *ESPN.com*. ESPN Internet Ventures, 26 Jan. 2004. Web. 11 Aug. 2012.

Simons, Steve. "Diamonds in The Rough." *Slam! Sports*. Canoe Inc., 28 May 2008. Web. 10 Aug. 2012.

St. James, Helene. "Red Wings' Datsyuk Puckish but Very Productive." *USA Today*. Gannett, 20 Jan. 2009. Web. 11 Aug. 2012.

—Bertha Muteba

Susan Desmond-Hellmann

Born: 1957
Occupation: Oncologist and translational scientist

Dr. Susan Desmond-Hellman was named the first female chancellor of the University of California, San Francisco (UCSF) on August 3, 2009. The school is among the top health-care training facilities in the United States, and Desmond-Hellmann is an alumna of the residency program there. After presiding over product development at the drug developer Genentech, where she oversaw the production of several of the most effective cancer-fighting drugs on the market, Desmond-Hellmann returned to UCSF to train a new generation of oncologists (as well as other physicians, researchers, and pharmacists). As Julian Guthrie wrote for the

Bloomberg via Getty Images

San Francisco Chronicle (11 Apr. 2010), Desmond-Hellmann's successes at Genentech have "made her a millionaire hundreds of times over," but she is far more interested in UCSF's potential to foster important and life-saving research than she is a paycheck.

Advancements in technology have led to better drugs for cancer patients, but the cost of research—among a host of other factors—has driven up prices on the most effective drugs, which has adversely affected patient treatment. One oncologist at the Mayo Clinic said that she avoided discussing a particular drug with patients she knew could not afford it. "I don't want them to feel bad," Dr. Angela Dispenzieri told Alex Berenson for the *New York Times* (12 July 2005). With the recent economic downturn, investment in biotechnologies is also down, but Desmond-Hellmann, who hopes to raise $100 million for UCSF by 2016, remains undeterred. Given the lack of funding for UCSF within the University of California (UC) system, Desmond-Hellmann is taking steps to make the school more autonomous by securing funding from a variety of new sources. She even began the fundraising initiative by donating $1 million of her own money. "We need to make drug development faster, cheaper, and more predictable," Desmond-Hellmann told Guthrie. "We need to get to the point where when a patient hears the words, 'You have cancer,' the patient also hears, 'And here is what we have for you.'"

Desmond-Hellmann, who spent two years conducting AIDS research in Uganda with her husband, has been the recipient of a number of awards and honors. When she was with Genentech, *Fortune* magazine listed her among the "Top 50 Most Powerful Women in Business" in 2001 and from 2003 to 2008. In 2007, she was inducted into the Biotech Hall of Fame. In 2005 and again in 2006, the *Wall Street Journal* selected Desmond-Hellmann for its annual "50 Women to Watch" list, and in 2009 she was awarded the Edison Achievement Award for leadership in innovation (past awardees include the late Steve Jobs of Apple and Ted Turner of Time Warner).

EARLY LIFE AND EDUCATION

The second of seven children, Desmond-Hellmann was born in 1957 in Napa, California, and was raised in Reno, Nevada. Her father, Frank Desmond, is a retail pharmacist who ran a Keystone Owl Rexall Drugstore when Desmond-Hellmann was growing up. Her mother, Jennie Desmond, is a breast cancer survivor (as is Desmond-Hellman's older sister) and a former English teacher.

Desmond-Hellmann worked as a bookkeeper in her father's pharmacy. She enjoyed watching him interact with customers, but it was the family physician, Dr. Noah Smirnoff, who impressed her with his bedside manner during a visit to treat her father when he had the flu. Before high school, she knew that she wanted to be a doctor. It was a career path that fit Desmond-Hellmann's self-described "nerdy" nature, which she felt was embraced and encouraged by her family. "There was a lot of emphasis on being a good student, on studying, and discussion about science and about medicine," she told Joanna Breitstein for the website PharmExec (1 Apr. 2006). "When I was growing up, I was very much the nerdy student. I admired people who were smart."

After graduating as valedictorian from her high school, Desmond-Hellmann enrolled in the University of Nevada, Reno, so that she could live at home and save money. She finished her undergraduate premedical degree in three years and stayed in Reno to earn her medical degree beginning in 1978. She planned to pursue sports medicine, but a month-long rotation with an oncologist named Dr. Stephen Hall at the Veterans Administration Hospital in Reno changed her mind. Desmond-Hellmann shifted her focus to internal medicine and then oncology.

When it came time to apply for an internship and a residency, UCSF was Desmond-Hellmann's first choice. Despite her stellar grades, winning a spot at UCSF was a long shot—most of the students in the applicant pool came from Ivy League schools. Lloyd "Holly" Smith, the former chair of the UCSF Department of Medicine, recalled Desmond-Hellmann's application to Guthrie: "Sue came from the University of Nevada, an institution we hadn't had any experience with. We took a chance on her because the university had written these letters filled with superlative descriptions. They said they had not seen a student like her."

Despite the support, Desmond-Hellmann felt like an underdog because of her background and gravitated toward another state-school student, Nick Hellmann from the University of Kentucky, who would later become her husband. Desmond-Hellmann distinguished herself by becoming board-certified in both internal medicine and oncology and serving as an assistant professor of hematology-oncology at UCSF. Like her husband—an infectious disease specialist—and a number of researchers in San Francisco during the 1980s, Desmond-Hellmann was concerned about the deadly AIDS epidemic. In particular, her concern focused on Kaposi's sarcoma, a viral cancer common in patients with AIDS. To educate herself about the epidemic and help fight it, she sought and earned a master's degree in public health in 1988 from the University of California, Berkeley.

UGANDA CANCER INSTITUTE AND PRIVATE PRACTICE

In 1989, Desmond-Hellmann and her husband received an offer from the Rockefeller Foundation, one of the oldest foundations devoted to public health, to study the heterosexual transmission of HIV/AIDS in Uganda. For two years, Desmond-Hellmann and her husband lived in Uganda where they conducted research at the Uganda Cancer Institute at Makerere University in Kampala, where they were also visiting faculty members. "It completely changed what I expected of myself," she told Carolyn Johnson of the experience in an interview for ABC 7 News, KGO-TV San Francisco (5 Apr. 2012). "I felt like I was so privileged and was incredibly fortunate compared to everyone I met in Uganda so I raised the personal bar of what I expected of myself in a powerful way."

The couple returned to the United States in 1991, and Desmond-Hellmann opened up a private oncology practice in her husband's home state of Kentucky. But Desmond-Hellmann was unsatisfied, particularly with the treatment options available to her patients. "We needed better weapons against cancer," she told a reporter for the journal *Nature Reviews: Drug Discovery* (July 2005), "and I wanted to be a part of that."

BRISTOL-MYERS SQUIBB

Upon returning to the United States, Hellmann's husband was offered a job with the biopharmaceutical company Bristol-Myers Squibb in Connecticut. In 1993,

Desmond-Hellmann began to work for the company as well. As associate director of clinical cancer research, she helped to develop the breast cancer drug Taxol (the same drug her mother would later use after being diagnosed with breast cancer). Taxol, officially approved by the Food and Drug Administration (FDA) to treat early stage breast cancer in 1998, was a breakthrough in what is known as "targeted drug" therapy, which "aimed at destroying tumors without the side effects of traditional chemotherapy," Berenson reported for the *New York Times* in 2005.

However, government officials and patients were outraged by the cost of Taxol, which in 1992 was $4,000 a year. Drug prices, particularly prices for anticancer drugs, have risen significantly since Taxol.

Still, Desmond-Hellmann was exhilarated by the difficult work, and in 1995, she was recruited by the biotechnology corporation Genentech in San Francisco.

GENENTECH

Desmond-Hellmann began her career with Genentech as a clinical scientist, where she applied the work of doctors Frederic de Sauvage, now the vice president of molecular biology at Genentech, and Dan Eaton, now the director of protein chemistry, to clinical study. De Sauvage and Eaton identified the hormone thrombopoietin as a key regulator of blood platelets. The resulting drug was unsuccessful, but Desmond-Hellmann quickly distinguished herself among her colleagues. Within a year of her hiring, she was put in charge of all clinical trials. After that, Arthur D. Levinson, the former CEO of Genentech and current chair of the board at Apple, told Guthrie: "Every six to twelve months, I was promoting her. Her instincts were excellent."

In 1999, Desmond-Hellmann became the executive vice president of development and product operations; in March 2004, she became president of product development. During her time at Genentech, the company became the number-one producer of anticancer drug treatments in the United States, largely thanks to her work and willingness to approach cancer treatments in a new way. The journal *Nature Reviews: Drug Discovery* wrote of Desmond-Hellmann's "try anything" attitude. The company that many considered to be an upstart in the pharmaceutical industry became the steward of a new era in cancer treatment. Of the early research that she saw to fruition, Desmond-Hellmann told Guthrie, "The period from 1997 to 2001 was an amazing time in oncology. It was a special time because there was such an unmet need." Among the drugs that Desmond-Hellmann and Genentech developed were the breast cancer drug Herceptin, which many consider to be her crowning achievement, and Avastin, which was originally developed to treat colon cancer. Other drugs that received FDA approval during Desmond-Hellmann's time with Genentech include Lucentis, which treats the "wet" form of macular degeneration; Tarceva, for advanced nonsmall cell lung cancer; Rituxan, for certain types of non-Hodgkin's lymphoma; and Xolair to treat allergy-related asthma.

> **We need to get to the point where when a patient hears the words, 'You have cancer,' the patient also hears, 'And here is what we have for you.'"**

DEVELOPMENT OF HERCEPTIN AND AVASTIN

The development of Herceptin was revolutionary because it was the first drug to target a particular mutation, associated with a specific type of breast cancer, in which cells overproduce a protein called HER2. Before the drug, the same treatments were applied to all patients with breast cancer, though researchers and doctors now understand that there are several distinct forms of the disease that require different, personalized therapies. HER2-positive breast cancer was considered to be one of the most deadly forms, but with Herceptin, it has become one of the most treatable. According to a number of sources, Desmond-Hellmann's father shares a story in which he and his wife, who was receiving chemotherapy at the time, overheard a doctor talking to another patient whose tumor had recurred. The doctor comforted the woman with "good news"; he was prescribing her an "incredible new drug called Herceptin." Pointing to Jennie Desmond, the doctor added, "You can thank the daughter of this lady for bringing it to you." The drug, like other anticancer medications, is expensive, however. Herceptin cost patients $20,000 per year in 1998, and according to several sources it can cost almost twice that today.

Avastin was the first drug to work by effectively blocking the blood cells that feed cancerous tumors. This restricts the tumor's growth and reduces the cancer's ability to spread to other areas of the body. Avastin, approved by the FDA to treat colon and lung cancer in 2006, was also approved through an accelerated approval process to treat metastatic breast cancer in 2008. The FDA revoked the latter decision in a 2011 split vote, citing potentially life-threatening risks that might outweigh the drug's benefits. Avastin remains on the market, however, and doctors and patients can still choose to use the drug to treat certain cancers.

CHANCELLOR OF UCSF

Genentech merged with the Swiss pharmaceutical giant Roche in March 2009. Desmond-Hellmann resigned her position with the company in April, though Roche executives reportedly asked her to stay. Later that year, on August 3, 2009, Desmond-Hellmann became the ninth chancellor of UCSF. During her first three years in the position, Desmond-Hellmann looked for ways to combat the school's increasing financial troubles with budget cuts while maintaining the funding necessary to run a research-based institution. Unlike its sister schools under the UC umbrella, UCSF does not have an undergraduate program, and tuition accounts for only 1 percent of the school's annual budget. (Most schools raise tuition or increase enrollment in the face of financial woes.) UCSF derives only 5 percent of its revenues from the state, finding most of its revenues from its patient-care services like medical centers, a children's hospital, and a number of clinics owned and operated by the school. The school received $532.8 million from the US National Institutes of Health in 2011, making UCSF the recipient of the largest grant among public institutions, second overall to the private research university Johns Hopkins University in Baltimore.

But with a state budget in disarray, shake-ups within the UC system had a negative impact on UCSF. In 2012, Desmond-Hellmann's team projected that the university will be losing money by 2015—the same year the school is scheduled to open a brand new medical center at Mission Bay. In January 2012, Desmond-Hellmann presented these figures to the regents of the nine UC branches. "What we have here," she said in reference to UCSF's current relationship to UC, as quoted by Nanette Asimov for the *San Francisco Chronicle* (20 Jan. 2012), "is not sustainable."

According to Asimov, Desmond-Hellmann further pointed out that UCSF devotes the most money to the UC system, yet sees the least in return. She also proposed her solution: a system in which UCSF maintains a more flexible relationship with UC, without seceding or becoming a private institution. If her proposal is accepted, UCSF would maintain its own board of directors.

Desmond-Hellmann has expressed an interest in partnering research facilities with pharmaceutical companies, and encouraging students to begin their own start-ups. "Increasingly, big biotech and big pharma are coming straight to academia for innovation. We're testing this," she told Kerry Dolan for *Forbes* (30 Apr. 2012). Desmond-Hellmann added that the school had already partnered with Pfizer. In addition to working directly with UCSF scientists, Pfizer provides funds for research projects. The program has been an experiment, Desmond-Hellmann noted. "I don't know if this will work," she told Dolan, "but we're going to test it and we're going to measure outcomes and I'm very convinced that Pfizer and others will come back for more if it is successful."

BOARD APPOINTMENTS AND PERSONAL LIFE

In addition to her work at UCSF, Desmond-Hellmann was appointed to the California Academy of Sciences board of trustees in 2008, and in 2009, she joined the Federal Reserve Bank of San Francisco's Economic Advisory Council for a three-year term. She served a three-year term as a member of the American Association for Cancer Research board of directors from 2005 to 2008. At the Biotechnology Industry Organization, Desmond-Hellmann served on the executive committee of the board of directors from 2001 until 2009. From 2004 to 2009, she served on the corporate board of the Santa Clara–based biotech company Affymetrix.

Desmond-Hellmann and her husband, who is currently the executive vice president of medical and scientific affairs at the Elizabeth Glaser Pediatric AIDS Foundation, were married in 1987. Desmond-Hellmann is a sports enthusiast; she skies, mountain bikes, and wakes up before five in the morning on weekdays to run.

SUGGESTED READING

Asimov, Nanette. "UCSF seeks to ease ties with UC." *San Francisco Chronicle*. Hearst Communications, 20 Jan. 2012. Web. 15 Sep. 2012.

Berenson, Alex. "Cancer Drugs Offer Hope, but at a Huge Expense." *New York Times*. New York Times, 12 July 2005. Web. 10 Sep. 2012.

Breitstein, Joanna. "HBA [Healthcare Businesswomen's Association] Woman of the Year: Susan Desmond-Hellmann." *PharmExec.com*. Advanstar Communications, 1 Apr. 2006. Web. 13 Sep. 2012.

Dolan, Kerry. "UCSF Chancellor Susan Desmond-Hellmann On How Healthcare is Changing." *Forbes*. Forbes, 30 Apr. 2012. Web. 9 Sep. 2012.

"From Uganda to San Francisco, the President of Product Development at Genentech describes her 'chaotic' career." *Nature Reviews: Drug Discovery*. Nature Publishing Group, July 2005. Web. 12 Sep. 2012.

Guthrie, Julian. "Cancer warrior takes the helm of UCSF." *San Francisco Chronicle*. Hearst Communications, 11 Apr. 2010. Web. 9 Sep. 2012.

Johnson, Carolyn. "UCSF chancellor honored by Commonwealth Club." *KGO-TV San Francisco*. ABC 7, 5 Apr. 2012. Web. 9 Sep. 2012.

—*Molly Hagan*

Peter Diamond

Born: April 29, 1940
Occupation: Economist and educator

Peter Diamond, an economics professor at the Massachusetts Institute of Technology (MIT), first came to widespread public attention in early 2010, when President Barack Obama nominated him for a seat on the Federal Reserve's Board of Governors. Later that year, he was awarded the Nobel Prize in economics for his "analysis of markets with search frictions," as his citation states. Given the approbation of the Nobel committee and the international acclaim being accorded Diamond, his supporters assumed that his seat on the Federal Reserve would be virtually assured. Republican lawmakers questioned his qualifications to serve on that body, however, and began to obstruct the proceedings. Diamond ultimately withdrew himself from consideration and wrote an

AP Photo

op-ed headlined "When a Nobel Prize Isn't Enough," which was published in the *New York Times* (5 June 2011). In the piece, he bemoaned the partisan bickering to which he had been subjected and wrote, "We should all worry about how distorted the confirmation process has become, and how little understanding of monetary policy there is among some of those responsible for its Congressional oversight."

EARLY LIFE AND EDUCATION

Diamond, a third-generation American, was born on April 29, 1940, in New York City. In many respects, his family's story is a classic tale of immigration, hard work, and eventual success. His maternal grandparents came to the United States from Poland at the beginning of the twentieth century, while his paternal grandparents hailed from Romania and Russia. His parents were born soon after their families settled in New York.

After graduating from high school, Diamond's parents began working. His mother found a job as a bookkeeper, earning fifteen dollars a week, and his father sold shoes during the day while getting a college education at night. He ultimately earned a degree from Brooklyn Law School, and in his early years of practice earned about five dollars a week. The couple married right before the Great Depression, and Diamond's older brother, Richard, was born in 1934.

Diamond lived and attended public school in the Bronx until he was in second grade, when he moved to the town of Woodmere, in suburban Long Island, with his family. Although the move to the suburbs was a step up socially and economically, the family's new home was so close to the Long Island Rail Road tracks that they woke to a train thundering by each day.

Diamond attended Yale University. Although he initially considered studying engineering, he soon settled upon math, studying game theory and topology. Exceedingly generous about paying tribute to teachers and other mentors, he has cited Shizuo Kakutani, one of his first math professors at Yale, as an influence. He has also credited Charles Berry with introducing him to economics. His mentor, Edward Budd, taught an economics honors seminar that was so compelling, Diamond dropped his French classes to take more economics courses. Diamond also studied with Gerard Debreu, who won a Nobel Prize in 1983.

Diamond graduated summa cum laude from Yale in 1960. In the summer of that year, he worked as a research assistant for another future laureate, Tjalling C. Koopmans, who won the Nobel Prize in 1975 for his work on the theory of resource allocation. Koopmans was responsible for Diamond's first publishing credit, listing Diamond as a cowriter on a 1964 paper titled "Stationary Utility and Time Perspective."

Diamond studied for his graduate degree at MIT, where he took courses in micro- and macroeconomics, statistics, economic history, and public finance. His thesis was supervised by Robert Solow, whom he considers a major role model. (Solow won the Nobel Prize in 1987, for his work on the theory of economic growth; the neoclassical Solow–Swan growth model is named, in part, for him.) In 1963, Diamond earned his doctoral degree in economics from MIT, and he was recruited to teach at University of California, Berkeley.

ACADEMIC CAREER

Diamond served as an assistant professor at Berkeley from 1963 to 1965, when he was appointed an acting associate professor. It was an exciting time to be at the school, which was an epicenter of political activism and the free-speech movement. Diamond taught micro- and macroeconomics and public finance, and he found his schedule, which allowed for a combination of research and teaching, to be exhilarating. While at Berkeley, he authored a well-received 1965 paper on the national debt and also spent time as a visiting fellow at the Churchill College, University of Cambridge.

In 1966, while he was in the United Kingdom, Diamond received an airmail letter from Solow, asking if he had any interest in joining the faculty of MIT. He accepted immediately and served as an associate professor from 1966 to 1970 and a full professor from 1970 to 1988, serving as the head of MIT's economics department from 1985 to 1986. In 1989, Diamond was named the John and Jennie S. MacDonald Professor, and he retained the title until 1992, when he became the inaugural holder of the Paul A. Samuelson chair, named for the MIT professor who is sometimes called the "father of modern economics." In 1997, Diamond stepped down from the prestigious chair to accept the title of institute professor, the highest possible professorship available at the school. MIT's institute professors are granted exceptional freedom to pursue their own research interests and are not required to teach, although Diamond has continued to do so, citing his love for imparting knowledge to his students and his belief that teaching complements and enriches his research.

In addition to his appointments at MIT, Diamond has been a visiting professor at several other schools, including University College in Nairobi (1968–69), Hebrew University in Jerusalem (1969), the University of Oxford's Nuffield College (1969) and Balliol College (1973–74), Harvard University (several times), the European University Institute (1992), and the University of Siena (2000).

MORE THAN AN ACADEMIC

Over the course of his career, Diamond has often focused on policy analysis rather than purely theoretical research. He has a particular interest in the subject of pensions. "Key to my work in this realm has been a series of enjoyable collaborations," he explained in an essay posted on the official Nobel Prize website. "This started serendipitously when, at the recommendation of Paul Samuelson, Bill [Hsiao] invited me to join the Panel on Social Security Financing consulting to the U.S. Senate Finance Committee, and I accepted. Pensions have been a perfect topic for me. They fit well in my public finance theory interests and with my social concerns. I have given many talks on Social Security, and ended some of them with a quote from Franklin Roosevelt, which I saw at his memorial in DC: 'The test of our progress is not whether we add more to the abundance of those who have much; it is whether we provide enough for those who have too little.'"

The work for which Diamond has won the greatest recognition is his research on "markets with search frictions"—markets in which buyers and sellers can have difficulty connecting with one another: those with used cars to sell and those needing reasonably priced transportation; landlords with apartments to rent and those seeking housing; and men looking for women to date and vice versa, for example.

In a piece for the *New York Times* (11 Oct. 2010), Harvard professor Edward Glaeser explained that Diamond's thoughts on the labor market—employers with jobs to fill and those searching for employment—were of great significance: "The most traditional economic model of the labor market assumes a labor supply schedule, which reflects the number of workers willing to work at a given wage, and a labor demand schedule, which describes the number of workers that companies are willing to hire at a given wage. At some wage, supply equals demand and that's the market equilibrium, which is where traditional economics predicts the world will end up. In markets with undifferentiated products—like copper or winter wheat—that model works pretty well, but it has some pretty obvious failings when it comes to labor or housing markets.

"In particular, the Economics 101 model does an awful job explaining an American civilian labor force where nearly one-tenth say they want a job and can't find one. . . . New paradigms emerge when reality crashes against theory, and that's what brought us [Diamond's] . . . search theory." Glaeser continued, "[Diamond's] work was distinguished both by elegant modeling—building the theoretical tools needed to make sense of labor turnover—and important insights. Perhaps the key idea is . . . that each 'additional worker makes it easier for vacancies to find workers and harder for other workers to find jobs.'" Diamond thus reasoned that the unemployed could congest the labor market, much as drivers congest a highway.

THE NOBEL PRIZE

In October 2010, it was announced that the Sveriges Riksbank Prize in Economic Sciences in Memory of Alfred Nobel was being awarded to Diamond, Dale T. Mortensen of Northwestern University, and Christopher A. Pissarides of the London School of Economics. Like Diamond, Mortensen and Pissarides had been researching markets with search frictions for decades. The three shared a cash prize of 10 million Swedish kroner (about $1.5 million). Glaeser echoed the sentiments of many observers when he wrote, "The prize

> *"I have given many talks on Social Security, and ended some of them with a quote from Franklin Roosevelt, which I saw at his memorial in DC: 'The test of our progress is not whether we add more to the abundance of those who have much; it is whether we provide enough for those who have too little.'"*

manages both to honor timeless research on core economic questions and to highlight the ways in which economics addresses a most timely global problem. . . .

"The work of these economists does not tell us how to fix our current high unemployment levels, but it does help us to make some sense of our current distress. . . ."

In addition to the Nobel, Diamond's many other honors include Guggenheim Fellowships (1966 and 1982), several National Science Foundation Research Grants (from 1965 to 2011), the Mahalanobis Memorial Award (1980), the Nemmers Prize (1994), a Fulbright Fellowship (2000), MIT's Killian Award (2003), the Jean-Jacques Laffont Prize (2005), the Robert M. Ball Award (2008), and an honorary doctoral degree from Hebrew University (2010). Additionally, he is a long-time fellow of both the Econometric Society and the American Academy of Arts and Sciences, as well as a founding member of the National Academy of Social Insurance, which is a nonpartisan, nonprofit organization devoted to educating the public about such programs as Social Security, Medicare, and workers' compensation.

THE FEDERAL RESERVE

In April 2010, President Obama nominated Diamond for a seat on the board of governors of the Federal Reserve, the central bank of the United States, which has as its mission "to provide the nation with a safer, more flexible, and more stable monetary and financial system." The Federal Reserve is chaired by Ben Bernanke, a former student of Diamond, and many political observers pointed out that the two would have a good working relationship.

In August of that year, however, Republican lawmakers took advantage of a little-used procedural rule and returned Diamond's nomination to the executive branch before summarily taking a summer recess. Political insiders in Washington, DC, posited that the nomination had been blocked in retaliation for the Democrats' treatment of Randall S. Kroszner, a George W. Bush appointee who stepped in to fill an unexpired term on the Federal Reserve board from 2006 to 2009 but was then denied a full fourteen-year term.

Leading the charge against Diamond was Senator Richard Shelby, the top-ranking Republican on the Senate Banking Committee, who was widely quoted as saying, "I do not believe he's ready to be a member of the Federal Reserve Board. I do not believe that the current environment of uncertainty would benefit from monetary policy decisions made by board members who are learning on the job" (qtd. in Klein).

In September 2010, Obama renominated Diamond for the post. The following month, when the Nobel Prize announcements were made, most political observers assumed that the prestigious award would sway Diamond's opponents and allow him to sail through the confirmation process. They did not count on the Republican's intransigence; Shelby and his compatriots, in a stance some journalists characterized as "anti-intellectual," asserted that winning the Nobel Prize was no qualification for holding one of the few coveted spots on the Federal Reserve's seven-member board of governors.

There was an understandable outcry from many quarters. In a June 6, 2011, article for the *Atlantic*, James Fallows expressed an opinion echoed in several other major outlets, writing, "Let's be serious. A career politician with a law degree from the University of Alabama. . . . [v]ersus the economist who has just been recognized with the highest international lifetime-achievement honor that exists in his field—and whose specialty is studying America's worst economic problem of the moment, chronic unemployment. Hmmm, I wonder which of them might be in a better position to judge the other's street-cred about Fed policy. Yet Senate rules let one willful politician say: No." Fallows continued, "Here's the real question. America is rich and resilient. But is it resilient enough to permit folly and self-destruction of this sort?"

In June 2011, Diamond informed the White House that he wanted his nomination withdrawn. In October 2011, Sarah Bloom Raskin, a former commissioner of financial regulation for Maryland, was appointed to the board in Diamond's stead.

DIAMOND'S BOOKS AND OTHER ACCOMPLISHMENTS

Diamond is the author and/or editor of several books, including: *Uncertainty in Economics, Readings, and Exercises* (1978); *Growth, Productivity, Unemployment: Essays to Celebrate Bob Solow's Birthday* (1990); *On Time: Lectures on Models of Equilibrium* (1994); *Social Security: What Role for the Future?* (1996); *Issues in Privatizing Social Security* (1999); *Social Security Reform* (2002); *Taxation, Incomplete Markets, and Social Security* (2002); *Saving Social Security: A Balanced Approach* (2004); *Behavioral Economics and Its Applications* (2007); *Reforming Pensions: Principles and Policy Choices* (2008); and *Pension Reform: A Short Guide* (2010).

From 1969 to 1971, Diamond was an associate editor of the *Journal of Economic Theory*, and he has held several editorial positions at the *Journal of Public Economics* and the *American Economic Review*. He chaired a study group for Kenya's Ministry of Planning in the late 1960s, and during the 1970s, he sat on advisory panels for the US Senate Finance Committee, the Congressional Research Service, and the National Commission on Social Security. He has held leadership posts with such groups as the Econometric Society and the American Economic Council and has been an associate of National Bureau of Economic Research since 1991.

PERSONAL LIFE

Diamond met his wife, Kate, while in Berkeley. They married in 1966, just ten days after he proposed. They have two sons: Matt, born in 1972, and Andy, born in 1979. The entire family accompanied Diamond to Stockholm on December 10, 2010, to witness his acceptance of the Nobel Prize.

The year 2010 also marked Diamond's seventieth birthday, which he celebrated by throwing out the ceremonial first pitch at Fenway Park, during a Boston Red Sox game. Kate had arranged the event, fulfilling one of her husband's long-held dreams. She also commissioned John Harbison to compose a piece of music in his honor titled "Diamond Watch: Double Play for Two Pianos."

SUGGESTED READING

Adams, Richard. "Peter Diamond's Nobel Prize in Economics Is All about Hard Work." *Guardian* [London]. Guardian News and Media, 11 Oct. 2010. Web. 10 Aug. 2012.

Diamond, Peter. "When a Nobel Prize Isn't Enough." *New York Times*. New York Times, 5 June 2011. Web. 10 Aug. 2012.

Fallows, James. "What's Wrong with America, Chapter 817: Sen. Richard Shelby." *Atlantic*. Atlantic Monthly Group, 6 June 2011. Web. 10 Aug. 2012.

Glaeser, Edward L. "The Work behind the Nobel Prize." *New York Times*. New York Times, 11 Oct. 2010. Web. 10 Aug. 2012.

Klein, Ezra. "Fourteen Reasons Why This Is the Worst Congress Ever." *Washington Post*. Washington Post, 13 July 2012. Web. 17 Sep. 2012.

—*Mari Rich*

Seth Grahame-Smith

Born: January 4, 1976
Occupation: Writer and producer

Seth Grahame-Smith first came to widespread attention with the publication of *Pride and Prejudice and Zombies* (2009), a best-selling book that is credited with kicking off the craze for literary "mash-ups," which combine two disparate elements or genres, often for comic effect. *Pride and Prejudice and Zombies,* for example, blends Jane Austen's formal prose style with that of pulp horror fiction. "It is a truth universally acknowledged, that a zombie in possession of brains must be in want of more brains," Grahame-Smith's book begins, echoing Austen's famed opening line about single men in possession of good fortunes being in want of wives.

Getty Images

The comic effect goes deeper, however, than mere syntax. "In the original book, England could be burning to the ground and all they would care about is who has the nicest silverware," Grahame-Smith told Oliver Good for the Abu Dhabi *National* (9 June 2009). "In this version, the country literally is falling apart around them, so it becomes that much more ridiculous and funny that they continue to obsess about gossip and relationships, even in the midst of a zombie uprising."

Grahame-Smith followed *Pride and Prejudice and Zombies* with *Abraham Lincoln: Vampire Hunter* (2010), a historical biography and horror hybrid that proved as popular as his Austen mash-up. "Grahame-Smith wasn't the first writer to put a bizarre spin on a classic tale (arguably, Shakespeare was a skilled practitioner of genre remixing). But he's become the mash-up movement's modern avatar," Alexandra Alter wrote for the *Wall Street Journal* (5 Apr. 2012). "His irreverent literary reboot landed at precisely the right cultural moment. In recent years, digital remixing and sampling—once viewed as derivative at best and illegal at worst—has grown widespread. . . . A zombie-infused Regency romance doesn't sound so ludicrous in today's mash-up rich environment."

In the wake of his literary success, Grahame-Smith has found himself much in demand in Hollywood—in the early part of 2012 alone his film adaptation of *Abraham Lincoln: Vampire Hunter* was released for the big screen, as was Tim Burton's *Dark Shadows*, the script for which he helped pen. In 2011, Grahame-Smith co-founded his own production company with partner David Katzenberg. He has few illusions that he is producing high art. "I understand exactly what I am," he told Alter. "I'm a big, bombastic novelist and thrill-ride guy. I'm never going to win the National Book Award."

EARLY LIFE AND EDUCATION

Grahame-Smith was born Seth Jared Greenberg on January 4, 1976, in Rockville Center, New York, though he was raised mainly in Connecticut. His father is Barry M. Greenberg, the founder of a company that facilitates celebrity participation in philanthropic or corporate events. His parents divorced when he was three. After the divorce, his mother, who worked as an editor at Connecticut-based publisher Marshall Cavendish, changed their last name to Grahame. According to most sources, she did so in homage to her favorite author, Kenneth Grahame, who is best known for the children's classic *The Wind in the Willows* (1908). Later, after she remarried, she adopted a hyphenated surname that incorporated her new husband's surname.

Grahame-Smith's stepfather was a dealer in used and rare books; the basement of the family home was filled with thousands of horror, fantasy, and science-fiction titles that he had collected. At an early age, Grahame-Smith became familiar with such writers as Robert Heinlein, Ray Bradbury, and Isaac Asimov. "But the real turning point for me came when I was 12, and [my stepfather] said, 'Okay, you're old enough for [Dean] Koontz and [Stephen] King,'" he told Ed Symkus for the *Boston Phoenix* (11 May 2002). "I worshipped at the altar of King, and have since then."

In 1994, Grahame-Smith graduated from Connecticut's Bethel High School, where he had been involved in the theater department. He subsequently studied at Emerson College in Boston, Massachusetts, where he participated in a film-production group called Frames Per Second and co-executive-produced the student awards show known as the EVVYs during his junior year.

AFTER GRADUATION

Upon earning his bachelor's degree in film in 1998, Grahame-Smith moved to Los Angeles, California, where he found work as a production assistant. His initial duties, according to some sources, consisted of fetching coffee and delivering dry cleaning for his employers. Eventually, he began writing narration and voice-over scripts for History Channel and Discovery Channel programming.

Concurrently, Grahame-Smith was writing in other formats away from the office. "I wrote one terrible manuscript after another for a decade and I guess they gradually got a little less terrible," he told Alix Sharkey for the London *Telegraph* (30 Apr. 2010). "But there were many, many unpublished short stories, abandoned screenplays and novels . . . a Library of Congress worth of awful literature." Given the responsibility of approving potential script ideas, he found himself listening to a seemingly endless stream of hopeful writers. It occurred to him that he belonged with them, on the more creative side of the process.

FIRST BOOKS

After quitting his job, Grahame-Smith began trying to cobble together a living as a freelance writer. He found regular work with Quirk Books, a Philadelphia-based publisher specializing in pop culture, humor, horror, and a category the company calls "irreference." His first assignment for the company was *The Big Book of Porn: A Penetrating Look at the World of Dirty Movies* (2005). He explained to Brad Moon for *Wired* magazine's "Geek Dad" column (17 Mar. 2010) that he was not embarrassed about working on the title. "If you were a struggling freelance writer and somebody said: 'We'll pay you to hang out on porn sets for six months, travel to conventions, go clubbing with the world's biggest porn starlets, watch a bunch of DVDs and write a funny book about it,' what would YOU say?"

Grahame-Smith published *The Spider-Man Handbook: The Ultimate Training Manual* in 2006, which includes chapters on how to treat a radioactive spider bite, take on a gang of henchmen, and crawl up a wall. Following that publication was another tongue-in-cheek instruction manual called *How to Survive a Horror Movie: All the Skills to Dodge the Kills* (2007), which covers such topics as how to perform an exorcism, survive a night of babysitting, persuade a skeptical local sheriff, and vanquish a murderous doll or possessed pet.

In 2008, Grahame-Smith published the novelty book *Pardon My President: Ready-to-Mail Apologies for 8 Years of George W. Bush: Just Tear and Send!*; the pages take the form of letters a reader could ostensibly rip out, sign, and send. For example, one missive, addressed to "the People of France," describes Republican congressman Bob Ney's 2003 call for all French fries sold in the US Capitol to be rebranded as "freedom fries," to express Ney's displeasure with France's opposition to the invasion of Iraq. The letter reads, "I apologize. You see, Mr. Ney is an idiot. If it's any consolation, a few years later he was sent to federal prison for corruption."

PRIDE AND PREJUDICE AND ZOMBIES

In 2009, Grahame-Smith heard from Jason Rekulak, an editor at Quirk Books. Rekulak had thought of a title for a book—*Pride and Prejudice and Zombies*—and needed a writer to take on the assignment. Grahame-Smith agreed and spent six weeks rereading Austen's 1813 novel, which is in the public domain, and revising it. "Austen wasn't very helpful," he joked to Carol Memmott for *USA Today* (5 Mar. 2010). "All she left me was the complete manuscript of one of the most beloved novels in the English language. I had to start on Page 1 and edit her work and weave in the zombie subplot that she had so carelessly forgotten."

Quirk initially published ten thousand copies of the book, expecting it to be only a modest success, but it debuted at number three on the *New York Times* best-seller list and quickly sold more than a million copies. Even many of Austen's most ardent fans and rigorous academicians were supportive. "I expected to be burnt at the stake; even to me it seemed slightly sacrilegious to rework one of the English language's greatest authors, but Austen lovers seem to have embraced it," Grahame-Smith told Sharkey. "I've had a lot of them tell me it's a great way to bring people into the Austen tent." *Pride and Prejudice and Zombies* has been optioned by Lionsgate Entertainment to be adapted into a film.

Not wanting to pigeonhole himself, Grahame-Smith turned down the chance to write another Austen mash-up; Quirk instead hired other writers to pen both a prequel to *Pride and Prejudice and Zombies* (*Dawn of the Dreadfuls*, 2010) and a sequel (*Dreadfully Ever After*, 2011).

ABRAHAM LINCOLN: VAMPIRE HUNTER

During his publicity tour for *Pride and Prejudice and Zombies*, Grahame-Smith noticed that several bookstores had set up displays for the upcoming two-hundredth anniversary of Abraham Lincoln's birth. Stephenie Meyer's *Twilight* book series (2005 to 2008), which focuses on a vampire and his human girlfriend, were at the height of their popularity at the time. "So next to every Lincoln table there would be a vampire table. Lincoln table, vampire table. Vampire table, Lincoln table," Grahame-Smith told Sharkey. The idea for his next mash-up presented itself to him immediately. "[Lincoln] didn't need vampires to make his life incredible, he was already an incredible guy. But if you add vampires, it's exponentially cooler," he explained. *Abraham Lincoln: Vampire Hunter* was published in 2010, earning its author a reported advance of $560,000, and landed quickly on the best-seller list.

Many historians and reviewers were impressed by the care that Grahame-Smith had taken with his subject matter and the sensitive way he had incorporated the themes of slavery and vampirism. "[T]his guy's on Mt. Rushmore, OK? He's on the $5 bill. He literally saved our nation from self-destruction," Grahame-Smith told Moon, explaining that during the course of his research, he had developed an even deeper respect for the nation's sixteenth president. "I intended vampire-hunting Abe to be the same brilliant, honest, idealistic self-made man he was in real life." Grahame-Smith was invited to give a reading at the Lincoln Presidential Museum in Springfield, Illinois;

> **"I understand exactly what I am. I'm a big, bombastic novelist and thrill-ride guy. I'm never going to win the National Book Award."**

afterward, the state historian escorted him into a temperature-controlled vault, lent him a pair of gloves, and allowed him to hold the handwritten manuscript of the "Gettysburg Address"—an honor very few people are ever accorded.

Grahame-Smith wrote the screenplay for a big-budget film version of his book, which premiered in June 2012. The film stars Benjamin Walker as an ax-wielding Lincoln, intent on ridding the nation of its scourge of vampires. In a review whose sentiments were echoed by many critics, Marc Savlov wrote for the *Austin Chronicle* (22 June 2012), "Set aside any preconceived notions you may have and let this inspired reworking of American history wash over you in all its gory, blood-red, exsanguinated-white, and bruised-blue glory."

UNHOLY NIGHT

Grahame-Smith's book *Unholy Night*, which was published in 2012, is a revisionist look at the three wise men present at the birth of Jesus. As he had done before starting his Lincoln book, the writer—who was born into a Jewish household and attended an Episcopalian church after his mother's remarriage—did intensive research. "That meant going back and reading the New Testament, reading the Gospel of Luke and Matthew . . . and researching the traditions that sprung up around the Wise Men in the ensuing centuries," he told Andy Lewis for the *Hollywood Reporter* (7 Apr. 2012). "It's interesting how there's . . . just a handful of lines [about them] really. They come from the East, they show up at Herod's, they burn incense and myrrh, they show up at the manger, and they leave never to be heard from again. Looking at the most famous birth story of all time: What if I could tell that through an unknown lens?"

Grahame-Smith imagines Balthazar, Melchyor, and Gaspar as fugitive thieves, who are forced to go on the run from Herod after burgling his palace. Happening upon Joseph, Mary, and their infant in a stable, the trio helps the young family escape to Egypt, as Herod's soldiers begin to slaughter each firstborn son in Judea.

While there was a minor outcry from the religious right, most critics appreciated the book. In a review for *Entertainment Weekly* (13 Apr. 2012), for example, Anthony Breznican praised Grahame-Smith's imagination and thought-provoking characterizations. "It's risky to turn a holy birth into a bloody sword-and-sandal yarn," he wrote, "but if you can forgive that, I bet you-know-who would." Grahame-Smith has also worked on a screenplay for a film version of the book.

OTHER SCREEN AND TELEVISION WORK

In 2010 Grahame-Smith and David Katzenberg created *The Hard Times of RJ Berger*, a raunchy teen sitcom that aired on MTV for two seasons. Grahame-Smith and Katzenberg discovered that they shared a comic sensibility and worked exceedingly well together. "I'm a juvenile 34, and David's a mature 27," Grahame-Smith told Dave Itzkoff for the *New York Times* (20 May 2010). "We kind of meet at 30 1/2."

The pair joined forces in 2011 to found KatzSmith Productions. The fledgling company signed a two-year deal that September with Warner Bros., and one of their first projects is reported to be a sequel to *Beetlejuice*, the 1988 Tim Burton hit about a ghost trying to drive a young couple out of their new home. Among their other possible projects are *Night of the Living*, an animated tale of monsters besieged by regular people; *Alive in Necropolis*, a supernatural crime thriller set in the real-life California town of Colma, which is home to a multitude of cemeteries; and *From Mia With Love*, a comedy about a group of awkward teenage boys who send for a Russian mail-order bride.

In addition to adapting his own books for the screen, in 2012 Grahame-Smith collaborated with director Tim Burton on *Dark Shadows*, which is based on a gothic soap opera of the same name. That program originally aired from 1966 to 1971 and has since enjoyed a loyal cult following. Although most reviewers found much to complain about, and the film was not the box-office success that had been predicted, Grahame-Smith was praised for his clever idea of setting the remake in the 1970s, a move that gave the recently resurrected vampire Barnabas Collins (played by Johnny Depp) several amusing lines and sight gags.

Grahame-Smith has been married since 2004 to Erin Stickle, a fellow Emerson College graduate. They have one son, Joshua, who was born in 2008. The family lives in Los Angeles.

SUGGESTED READING

Alter, Alexandra. "The Master of the Mash-Up." *Wall Street Journal*. Dow Jones & Co., 5 Apr. 2012. Web. 16 Aug. 2012.

Babayan, Siran. "Seth Grahame-Smith's New Book *Unholy Night* Asks: What the Hell Were the Three Wise Doing There?" *LA Weekly*. LA Weekly, 6 Apr. 2012. Web. 20 June 2012.

Good, Oliver. "Corpse Pride." *National* [Abu Dhabi]. Abu Dhabi Media, 9 June 2009. Web. 16 Aug. 2012.

Itzkoff, Dave. "A Standout Student at Ribald High." *New York Times*. New York Times Co., 20 May 2010. Web. 16 Aug. 2012.

Lewis, Andy. "Seth Grahame-Smith Touts New Novel 'Unholy Night,' Discusses Movie Schedule and Collaborating With Tim Burton (Q&A)." *Hollywood Reporter*. Hollywood Reporter, 7 Apr. 2012. Web. 16 Aug. 2012.

Memmott, Carol. "Q&A with Seth Grahame-Smith, Master of the Mashup." *USA Today*. Gannett Co. Inc., 5 Mar. 2010. Web. 16 Aug. 2012.

Sharkey, Alix. "Seth Grahame-Smith Interview." *Telegraph* [London]. Telegraph Media Group, 30 Apr. 2010. Web. 16 Aug. 2012.

Symkus, Ed. "Interview: Seth Grahame-Smith Emerges from the Shadows." *Boston Phoenix*. Phoenix Media/Communications Group, 11 May 2012. Web. 16 Aug. 2012.

—*Mari Rich*

Matthew Herbert

Born: 1972
Occupation: Electronic musician, producer, and composer

British electronic music artist Matthew Herbert "has done more for the possibilities of sampling culture than any other artist currently at work," Dimitri Nasrallah wrote for the monthly Canadian music magazine *Exclaim!* (Nov. 2008). "Whether he's chopping up food for sound, leading big bands, writing manifestos, railing against globalization, or simply making dance music out of bodily functions," Nasrallah

Redferns via Getty Images

noted, "Matthew Herbert has consistently taken his music into corners other people couldn't even imagine. Like Brian Eno, he's eclectic, wildly creative, and eager to collaborate with a wide range of musicians and musical styles." Herbert, the founder of the independent label Accidental Records and creator of an influential manifesto called the "Personal Contract for the Composition of Music (Incorporating the Manifesto of Mistakes)," or PCCOM manifesto, has been recording and performing professionally under a variety of aliases, including Wishmountain, Doctor Rockit, Herbert, Radio Boy, and the Matthew Herbert Big Band, since the mid-1990s. Under those aliases Herbert has released nearly two dozen full-length albums and countless other EPs and singles covering a diverse range of styles, including house, techno, pop, classical, big band, jazz, and funk. He is known particularly for his sampling prowess and pioneering use of found sounds in electronic dance music, which have helped him become one of the most in-demand remixers and producers in the music industry. He is also known for his strong political views, which have inspired many of his musical compositions.

EARLY LIFE AND EDUCATION

Herbert was born in 1972 and grew up in the village of Five Oak Green, in Kent, a county in southeastern England. His father worked as a sound engineer for the British Broadcasting Corporation (BBC) and his mother was a teacher; he has a sister, whose name has not been publicized. Herbert developed a fascination with music at an early age, largely through the influence of his father, who started him on piano and violin lessons when he was four years old. "He would always be taking something apart," he said of his father to Dimitri Nasrallah, adding, "Seeing the insides of a radio was just as much of influence as what came out of it." Herbert was raised in a strict Methodist household and grew up without a television. As a result he spent much of his childhood playing various instruments, listening to the radio, and leading other isolated pursuits. Early on Herbert developed alternative musical tastes through the radio, becoming a fan of such artists as the groundbreaking German electronic-music band Kraftwerk and the American avant-garde singer-songwriter Tom Waits. He told Larry Fitzmaurice for the music website Pitchfork (13 Feb. 2012), "For me, music was a little window into an alternative world. And when your diet is mainstream music, you become very receptive to anything that deviates from that."

Naturally musically gifted, Herbert started playing in school orchestras and choirs when he was seven years old. By the time he reached his teens, he was playing a variety of instruments in different bands, among which included a twenty-five-piece, Glenn Miller–style big band jazz ensemble. At sixteen, Herbert toured Europe for the first time with one of the orchestras he was involved with. During this time his musical interests expanded to include psychedelic rock, hip-hop, and aleatoric music, or music in which some elements are left to chance. Herbert was greatly influenced by a school music teacher, Pete Stollery. Stollery introduced Herbert to the work of the American composer Steve Reich, whose 1966 piece "Come Out to Show Them," about the 1964 Harlem riots, made innovative use of found sounds and tape loops. After listening to "Come Out," Herbert explained to Nasrallah, "That's when I realized that music wasn't just scales or something you did for an hour a week with a slightly scary violin teacher. It was political, it was electronic, futuristic somehow, if that's the appropriate word, it's challenging, beautiful, airy, and it's unique as well. It was something I'd never heard before in that way."

UNIVERSITY AND THE RAVE SCENE

Herbert studied drama at England's Exeter University in the early 1990s. By that time he had accumulated enough electronics equipment to set up his own home recording studio. At Exeter Herbert became fascinated by the relationship between music and performance and started recording and sampling everyday sounds from his surroundings to include in his drama compositions. It was during this time that he discovered the burgeoning British rave scene, which spawned different genres and subgenres of electronic dance music. Growing fond of house music, Herbert started deejaying at raves and other venues around England. He soon developed a following and began creating dance music assembled from his growing catalog of found sounds under the moniker Wishmountain. Herbert's original and forward-thinking musical style helped him catch the attention of the now-defunct dance music label Mighty Force, which was best known for releasing works by the electronic music performer Aphex Twin (the stage name of Richard D. James). According to Herbert's website, the label released his first production credit, a collaborative EP called *Monster Magnet* (under the guise of Fog City), in 1993. Herbert went on to collaborate with other artists, including the British production duo Global Communication. By the time he graduated from Exeter University, in 1994, he was recording and performing diverse styles of music under an array of aliases.

EARLY CAREER

After college, Herbert moved to London to pursue his career in music full-time, a decision inspired by the death of a close friend in 1994. He told David Stubbs, in a biography posted on Herbert's website, "This death was the impetus to push on with my music. It's the silent powerplant at the heart of my work." Herbert gave his first major public performance as Wishmountain in January 1995, at the Arches nightclub in Glasgow, Scotland, for which he performed a live deejay set using only a sampler and a bag of potato chips. The set was well received and prompted him to sample and rework numerous other everyday objects during subsequent live sets. (Herbert has published a sonography on his website detailing all of the sounds he has recorded over the course of his career.) Also in 1995 Herbert released his first full-length album—*Ready to Rockit*—as Doctor Rockit, on the Clear label. The album featured an "electro-jazzy sound with vocal snippets," as was noted in *The Rough Guide to Rock* (2003), which was edited by Peter Buckley.

Herbert's profile rose considerably in 1996, with the release of a number of projects under his Wishmountain, Doctor Rockit, and Herbert monikers. That year saw him release his first Wishmountain EP, Radio, on Universal Language Productions; his second full-length effort as Doctor Rockit, The Music of Sound, on Clear; and debut album as Herbert, 100lbs, on Phono Records, which featured material compiled from a series of EPs. As Herbert, his music was rooted largely in the house genre, characterized by the heavy use of samples and repetitive four-to-the-floor, or 4/4, rhythms, which stood in contrast

> *"For me, music was a little window into an alternative world."*

to the sonic experimentalism of Wishmountain and electro-based sound of Doctor Rockit. David Stubbs wrote that 100lbs "feels very much a Herbert album . . . self-consciously assembled, precisely weighted, sleek, sending micro-fragments showering and skittering across its own, silvery surfaces yet plumbing Moog House depths." Herbert would record under yet another alias—Radio Boy—in 1997, when he released the album Long Live Radio Boy on the Antiphon label.

RADIO BOY AND HERBERT

In 1998, Herbert released the album *Wishmountain is Dead—Long Live Radio Boy*, on Antiphon, marking his last effort under the name Wishmountain, which he abandoned in favor of Radio Boy. As Dimitri Nasrallah puts it, "The Radio Boy alias pursues the same experimental sampling ethos of Wishmountain, but with a more direct political stance in mind, reflecting the rising importance of politics in Herbert's views and the continued influence of the early sampling politics embedded in Steve Reich's compositions." In the same year, Herbert released another album under the Herbert moniker, *Around the House,* on the Phonography label. For that album, which was critically well received, Herbert turned away from using samples of other people's music in favor of sounds of everyday, household objects such as kitchen sinks and washing machines, which he sampled into accessible house rhythms. The album featured vocals by his then-girlfriend and eventual first wife, the jazz singer Dani Siciliano (whom he had met while touring in San Francisco), who sang on such tracks as "So Now" and "We Still Have (The Music)." In a review of *Around the House* for the AllMusic website, John Bush made note of Herbert's "deep liquid basslines and staccato kitchen-sink percussion" and praised Siciliano's "languorous vocals." (*Around the House* was rereleased on the !K7 label in 2002.)

By the late 1990s Herbert had started contributing music to film soundtracks, including director Justin Kerrigan's comedy *Human Traffic* (1999). He had also become an in-demand remixer working on songs for a wide range of artists, including Spacetime Continuum, Agent Blue, Moloko, Atom Heart, Motorbass, Furry Phreaks, Sven Vath, Presence, and Visit Venus.

HERBERT'S MANIFESTO

In 2000 Herbert released a mix album of his own called *Let's All Make Mistakes*, which included songs by such techno artists as Plastikman, Theo Parrish, and Green Velvet, as well as five original productions. That same year he founded the independent label Accidental Records and wrote a manifesto, titled "Personal Contract for the Composition of Music (Incorporating the Manifesto of Mistakes)"—or PCCOM manifesto—which featured a list of eleven artistic principles that would provide a template for much of his subsequent work. Herbert's manifesto forbids the use of drum machines, synthesizers, prerecorded sounds, and the sampling of other people's work, while encouraging accidents and randomness in the recording process. Calling his decision to create the manifesto "entirely sudden," Herbert, who by that time had become fed up with the ideologically vacant house music scene, explained to Stubbs, "It was an exciting realisation—that the artistic agenda in electronic music was there for the taking. I don't mean that in an arrogant way, but in a practical way. There has never been any magazine or place for people to talk about music in the way I was brought up to talk about art, literature, film, etc." Herbert's PCCOM manifesto has drawn comparisons to the Danish filmmaker Lars von Trier's Dogme 95 Manifesto, which features a set of rules about filmmaking.

THE MECHANICS OF DESTRUCTION AND *BODILY FUNCTIONS*

In 2001 Herbert released two of his most overtly political albums, *The Mechanics of Destruction* and *Bodily Functions*, under his Radio Boy and Herbert monikers, respectively. The former tackled the theme of globalization and corporate greed through the use of sounds culled entirely from wasteful consumer products, featuring samples of everything from a McDonald's Big Mac ("McDonalds") to Rupert Murdoch's the *Sun* newspaper ("Rupert Murdoch"). Herbert gave away *The Mechanics of Destruction* for free via download on his website, as a way to further drive home the album's message. Meanwhile, for *Bodily Functions*, he centered on the theme of human relationships by using samples taken mostly from the human body, which were set "against a jazzy house backdrop," as Jonathan Wingfield noted for the *New York Times* (10 Mar. 2010). This album again featured Dani Siciliano on vocals. Herbert described *Bodily Functions* to Nasrallah as "a political album about relationships and feeling alienated from the state, about the alienation that begins to crop up in personal lives once corporations begin popping up everywhere."

THE MATTHEW HERBERT BIG BAND

Herbert next reinvented himself as the leader of the Matthew Herbert Big Band, with the album *Goodbye Swingtime*, which was released on Accidental in 2003. For the album, which was recorded at the famous Abbey Road Studios, he assembled a full swing orchestra made up of sixteen British jazz musicians, including trombonist Gordon Campbell, saxophonist Nigel Hitchcock, bassist Dave Green, and pianist Phil Parnell; the band was rounded out by Dani Siciliano and other performers. Like *The Mechanics of Destruction* and *Bodily Functions*, *Goodbye Swingtime* was made under the guidelines set forth in the PCCOM manifesto and carried a political message. It featured elaborate big band orchestrations (all written by Herbert) set to politically inspired sounds, such as percussive beats made by dropping phonebooks or paging through political books written by Noam Chomsky and Michael Moore, as a way to criticize the 2003 invasion of Iraq. The Matthew Herbert Big Band would subsequently perform at jazz festivals all over the world. In 2008 Herbert reconvened the band for a follow-up album—*There's Me and There's You*—which featured the London-based session singer Eska and dealt with the theme of overconsumption.

PLAT DU JOUR

Herbert concentrated on the subject of food for 2005's *Plat du Jour*—released as Matthew Herbert—which was assembled from a large collection of sounds related to food preparation, production, and consumption. Among its tracks included "The Truncated Life of a Modern Industrialised Chicken," which had a recording of thirty thousand broiler chickens in a barn; "An Empire of Coffee," which incorporated the thud of sixty Vietnamese coffee beans being dropped into a can of weedkiller; "Sugar," which included the sound of a can of Coca-Cola; and "An Apple a Day . . .," which featured an audio sample of more than three thousand people eating an apple. In conjunction with the release of *Plat du Jour*, Herbert launched the website Plat du Jour, which provided in-depth information about the two-and-a-half-year making of the album. For his accompanying live show, he performed alongside a brigade of chefs. As noted on the Accidental Records website, a writer for the London *Guardian* called the resultant live shows "a wild stimulation of senses, feet, and intellect."

SCALE

In 2006 Herbert released the album *Scale* (as Herbert) on the !K7 label. Inspired by funk and disco, the album featured eleven tracks that incorporated the sounds of more than six hundred objects, among which included bells, coffins, and petrol pumps. It was both a critical and commercial success and was Herbert's first album to reach the Top 20 on *Billboard*'s electronic music album chart. *Scale* also marked his last collaboration with Dani Siciliano, who sang on ten of the album's eleven tracks. (The two would separate following the recording of the album.) Andy Kellman, in a review of the album on the website AllMusic, commented, "Herbert is more upset about the state of the planet than ever, especially when it comes to the actions and inactions of Bush and Blair, but he has also made it known that he aimed to make an enjoyable, richly musical album full of melodies and multi-part harmonies." He added that its songs "are unmistakably his and Siciliano's, sounding like no one else, twisting and swinging and drifting with optimum vibrancy. Some of them are big and bold enough to be used in a stage production. All of them are 100 percent heavenly, even when they're dealing with loss."

THE "ONE" TRILOGY

Score, compilation of Herbert's unreleased film scores, was released on !K7 in 2007. He has since recorded a trilogy of albums—*One One*, *One Club*, and *One Pig*—the first two of which were released in 2010 and the third in 2011. All three albums, known as the "One" trilogy, were released on Accidental Records under the name Matthew Herbert. For the first installment, which tracks a day in the life of a single man, Herbert wrote and performed every piece of music himself, and for the second, he used samples taken from one night at the Robert Johnson club in Frankfurt, Germany. The third is based on the life and eventual slaughter of a pig on a farm in the British countryside. Although *One Pig* began drawing complaints from the animal rights organization People for the Ethical Treatment of Animals (PETA) more than a year before its release, Herbert has said that the album is meant to reflect on the harsher realities in everyday life. "The pig is simply the most divisive of all animals," he told Ben Sisario for the *New York Times* (17 Oct. 2011). "You probably come into contact with a pig product 10 or 20 times in one day, from ink jet paper to a glass of milk. And yet they're the subject of so much scorn and contempt. I think it's strange that we've built a society that's so dependent on something, and yet we rarely give it a voice of its own." He added, "The most important message of a lot of my projects is that I would like us to listen to the world a little more carefully."

MOST RECENT ALBUMS AND COLLABORATIONS

Herbert's other recordings include *Mahler Symphony X*, a reinterpretation of the Austrian composer Gustav Mahler's tenth symphony. The album was released on the Deutsche Grammophon label in 2010, and the score to the 2011 YouTube documentary film *Life in a Day*, which he made in collaboration with the British composer Harry Gregson-Williams. In addition to remixing hundreds of songs, Herbert has produced albums for several artists, including the Irish singer-songwriter Róisín Murphy's solo debut *Ruby Blue* (2005), the British band the Invisible's Mercury Prize–nominated self-titled debut (2008), the British singer-songwriter Micachu's debut *Jewelry* (2008), and the British pop artist Rowdy Superstar's debut *Battery* (2010). He worked as a programmer on the Icelandic singer-songwriter Björk's album *Vespertine* (2001), and has collaborated with the likes of such high-profile musicians as Quincy Jones, Dizzee Rascal, Ennio Morricone, R.E.M., Perry Farrell, Yoko Ono, and John Cale of the Velvet Underground. He has also composed music for various dance companies and theaters. To date, he has performed numerous sold-out shows at venues on four continents around the world.

Herbert is divorced from his longtime collaborator Dani Siciliano. He has since remarried and has a son.

SUGGESTED READING

Birchmeier, Jason. "Matthew Herbert: Biography." *AllMusic*. Rovi Corp., 2012. Web. 18 July 2012.

Fitzmaurice, Larry. "Matthew Herbert: The Avant-Electronic Explorer on Kraftwerk, Tom Waits, De La Soul, and More." *Pitchfork*. Pitchfork Media Inc., 13 Feb. 2012. Web. 18 July 2012.

Hodgkinson, Will. "Big Bang." *Guardian* 30 Oct. 2003: 26. Web. 18 July 2012.

Nasrallah, Dimitri. "Herbert: Pitch Control." *Exclaim.ca*. Exclaim! Magazine, Nov. 2008. Web. 18 July 2012.

Richardson, Mark. "Interviews: Matthew Herbert." *Pitchfork*. Pitchfork Media Inc., 10 July 2006. Web. 18 July 2012.

Sisario, Ben. "Raising an Album, from Pigpen to Studio." *New York Times*. New York Times Co., 17 Oct. 2011. Web. 18 July 2012.

Stubbs, David. "Matthew Herbert Biography." *Matthew Herbert*. Matthew Herbert, 2011. Web. 18 July 2012.

Welsh, April. "Matthew Herbert's One Pig Project." *Independent*. independent.co.uk, 22 Aug. 2011. Web. 18 July 2012.

Wingfield, Jonathan. "Bring in Da Noise." *New York Times*. New York Times Co., 10 Mar. 2010. Web. 18 July 2012.

—Chris Cullen

Rosamund Pike

Born: January 27, 1979
Occupation: Actress

Since her breakout movie debut as the beautiful and devious Miranda Frost in the James Bond film *Die Another Day* (2002), British stage and screen star Rosamund Pike has developed into one of the United Kingdom's more versatile and accomplished actresses. Pike fuses natural charisma with an acting talent that she has honed since childhood. Though Pike has played the lead in a number of theatrical productions on the British stage, depicting Alma in Tennessee Williams's *Summer and Smoke* and the title characters in Terry Johnson's *Hitchcock*

Getty Images

Blonde, Yukio Mishima's *Madame de Sade*, and Henrik Ibsen's *Hedda Gabler*, she is known principally for her supporting roles in such films as *The Libertine* (2004), *Pride and Prejudice* (2005), *Fracture* (2007), *An Education* (2009), *Barney's Version* (2010), *Made in Dagenham* (2010), *Wrath of the Titans* (2012), and the forthcoming *Jack Reacher* (2013). As Ann Hornaday observed for the *Washington Post* (28 Jan. 2011), Pike "has become something of a best-kept secret among discerning viewers. General audiences may not know her name, but they may well have found themselves captivated by her un-showy but indelible supporting performances."

EARLY LIFE

Rosamund Mary Elizabeth Pike was born January 27, 1979, in London, England, the only child of Julian Pike, an opera singer (and now the head of vocal and operatic studies at the Birmingham Conservatoire, in Birmingham, England), and Caroline Friend Pike, an opera singer and concert violinist. Though raised in London, Pike spent much of her youth traveling with her parents whose musical careers took them all over Europe. Despite the apparent glamour, the Pikes were not wealthy. "We often didn't have much money, but [my parents] loved their work and that kind of made everything else worthwhile for them. I felt secure in every other way, though," Pike told Stuart Husband for the *Observer* (12 Oct. 2002).

The early introduction to the world of drama and the arts left an impression on Pike and steered her toward her future career. "I spent quite a lot of time in rehearsal rooms or in the wings, looking at [my parents] being the stars," she commented to Lynn Barber for the *Observer* (23 May 2009). "It was definitely what gave me the bug, seeing my mum playing the Merry Widow—it's a wonderful opera—and she had this boa and a big wig, and looked just gorgeous: like a film star, I thought. I was a bit of a frumpy child and she just looked incredibly glamorous and exciting."

Belying her youth, Pike displayed an early dedication to acting as a calling and, thanks in part to the artistic exposure she received as a child, developed a precocious perception that helped her grow into her craft. "I was weirdly serious about [acting] from very young, about 10 or something," she remarked to Barber. "And watching my parents, there was a real analytical interest in what made something believable and what made it not believable, or what made something moving or funny, or why these lines didn't ring true."

EDUCATION

In 1990, at the age of eleven, Pike earned a scholarship to the prestigious Badminton School, an all-girls boarding academy in Bristol, England. Throughout her time at Badminton, Pike found it difficult to fit in among her wealthy classmates. As a young teenager, she recalled herself as a bit of an ugly duckling, far from the glamorous beauty she would become. Nevertheless, Pike's commitment to acting did not diminish. She took part in a number of school plays and, due to her height, she often performed the male roles. At sixteen, she was accepted into the National Youth Theatre, a training ground for the United Kingdom's most promising young actors. Two years later, she played Juliet in the organization's production of William Shakespeare's *Romeo and Juliet*.

Pike did exceptionally well on her university entrance exams and after graduating from Badminton in 1997, went on to Wadham College, Oxford University. There she studied English and took part in various dramatic productions staged at the school. She also made her television debut, appearing in a supporting role in the film *A Rather English Marriage* (1998), which was broadcast by the British Broadcasting Corporation (BBC). The following year she appeared in several episodes of the BBC miniseries *Wives and Daughters*.

As her acting ambitions overshadowed her academic ones, Pike made the decision to focus exclusively on her passion. She dropped out of Wadham and applied to a number of drama schools. Despite her strong credentials, "I got rejected from them all," Pike informed Lucy Cavendish for the *Telegraph* (18 Mar. 2009). "It was very hard to take. I had to crawl back to Wadham and beg to be allowed to finish my degree." The overwhelming rejection was hard for her to reconcile. In hindsight, the reasons for her lack of success were complicated. As she explained to Judith Woods for the *Mail* (24 Sep. 2010), "Later I met someone who had been on one of the panels, and he admitted I'd done the best audition he'd ever seen but he'd been overruled because his colleagues felt I was born with a silver spoon in my mouth, which simply isn't true." Despite her relatively modest upbringing, Pike's private school education, upper-class accent, and stunning appearance led people to erroneous conclusions about her background. "There's this impression that I've somehow lived a charmed life," Pike explained to Woods. "I wouldn't mind being thought of as privileged if I'd had any of the wealth that's supposed to accompany it, but we weren't at all well off."

BOND GIRL

As she finished up her studies at Oxford, Pike landed several small roles on British television in 2000 and 2001. She graduated from Wadham in 2001, earning an upper second class honors degree, the equivalent of graduating magna cum laude in the United States. After completing school, she went on auditions while also looking for a job. She acted in an episode of the British police procedural *Foyle's War* in 2002, but a truly breakout role eluded her. As she weighed whether to accept a position at the Waterstones bookstore chain, she auditioned for *Die Another Day*, starring Pierce Brosnan, Halle Berry, and Judi Dench. Pike read for the role of Miranda Frost, an Olympic fencer and double agent who becomes romantically involved with Bond. Pike did not think she had a serious chance of landing the part and left the audition with few illusions, heading off to an isolated cottage in Lincolnshire. The house had no phone, so she had no idea that everyone on the film, including the director Lee Tamahori, was trying to get a hold of her for the first of many callbacks. After numerous screen tests, "They told me, you're the Bond girl," Pike recollected to Woods. "And I was completely speechless. It hit me: it's like becoming part of movie history."

Though *Die Another Day* received mixed reviews, the film was a box office smash, grossing over $400 million worldwide. For Pike, *Die Another Day* propelled her to international stardom. As Lucy Cavendish noted in the *Telegraph* (19 Mar. 2009), "She seemed to come from absolutely nowhere yet was received with rapturous attention by audiences worldwide." The role earned her a 2003 Empire Award for best newcomer from the British film magazine *Empire*.

After *Die Another Day*, rather than pursue more film work, Pike opted instead for the stage, accepting the title role in *Hitchcock Blonde*, which premiered on London's West End, at the Royal Court Theatre, in the spring of 2003. The play is set variously in the years 1999, 1959, and 1919 and explores the legendary filmmaker Alfred Hitchcock's on-screen obsession with blonde women. Pike played the body double of the actress Janet Leigh during the filming of Hitchcock's *Psycho* (1960) and its iconic shower sequence. The role was a difficult one, involving a prolonged nude scene, where for ten minutes Pike wore nothing except a pair of high heels.

FILM ROLES

Pike returned to the silver screen in 2004, appearing in two pictures, the Amos Gitai–directed *Promised Land* and *The Libertine*, starring Johnny Depp. A French-Israeli film, *Promised Land* depicted sex trafficking in Israel. While reviews for the film varied among the English-speaking press, *Promised Land* was honored at the 2004 Venice Film Festival with a special prize for its promotion of peace.

In *The Libertine*, directed by Laurence Dunmore, Pike played Elizabeth Malet, the long-suffering wife of John Wilmot, the Earl of Rochester, and the film's title character. A seventeenth-century poet and satirist with ties to England's King Charles II, Rochester was famous, too, for his drunken debauchery and early death. With few exceptions, *The Libertine* did not fare well critically. Pike's performance stood out, however. Alison Jane Reid, writing for the *Independent* (3 Dec. 2005), described Pike's Elizabeth as a "heart-breaking portrait of love

> *"I want to be respected, so that to have my name attached to a project means something. Obviously it would be great to do some wonderful enriching roles, but I want to just carry on doing it all my life. Because [acting] just keeps you so young, it keeps you so fulfilled—it's the most fulfilling job in the world, really."*

and loyalty betrayed as the stoic consort of Johnny Depp's Rochester." At the 2005 British Independent Film Awards, Pike captured the best supporting actress honor.

Pike took the role of Jane Bennet in *Pride and Prejudice*, Joe Wright's adaptation of the 1813 Jane Austen novel. The film stars Keira Knightley as Elizabeth Bennet and Matthew Macfadyen as Mr. Darcy and centers on various efforts to see the five Bennet sisters successfully married off. The film, Stephen Holden wrote for the *New York Times* (11 Nov. 2005), "gathers you up on its white horse and gallops off into the sunset. Along the way, it serves a continuing banquet of high-end comfort food perfectly cooked and seasoned to Anglophilic tastes. In its final minutes, it makes you believe in true love, the union of soul mates, happily-ever-after and all the other stuff a romantic comedy promises but so seldom delivers." Alison Jane Reid described Pike performance as "supremely intelligent."

While working on the set of *Pride and Prejudice*, Pike was offered a role in *Doom* (2005), a science fiction film based on the video game of the same name. "When I got the call about *Doom*, I was in a bonnet in a field near Tunbridge Wells. I thought: 'My God, if they could see me—they would probably recast!'" Pike informed James Nottram for *Metro* (27 Oct. 2009). Pike played Dr. Samantha Grimm, a forensic archaeologist, stationed on Mars who meets up with a detachment of space marines sent to the planet to investigate strange happenings at a research lab where they encounter a host of deadly creatures. "*Doom* was a truly dreadful film," Pike told a writer for the *Scotsman* (2 Oct. 2009). "It was beset by certain problems. At one stage, we really thought it would be quite brilliant and edgy."

ON STAGE AND SCREEN

Following a return to the stage as Alma in Tennessee Williams's *Summer and Smoke,* which opened at London's Apollo Theatre in 2006, Pike appeared with Anthony Hopkins and Ryan Gosling in the legal suspense thriller *Fracture*. Playing corporate attorney Nikki Gardner, Pike becomes romantically involved with Gosling's character, Willie Beachum, a district attorney looking to make a lucrative transition into private practice—if he can just put one puzzling murder case to rest.

Pike next played a supporting role in the Holocaust drama *Fugitive Pieces* (2007), adapted from the Anne Michaels novel. Pike's character, Alex, is the wife of Jakob Beer, portrayed by Stephen Dillane, a young Holocaust survivor who after seeing his family slaughtered by the Nazis in Poland escapes to Greece and then to Canada, where he becomes a writer and teacher. Haunted by his past, Jeannette Catsoulis observed for the *New York Times* (2 May 2008), "Jakob remains shackled to memories that draw him ever inward and repel his high-spirited young wife, Alex (a touching Rosamund Pike)." The role earned Pike a Genie Award nomination for best supporting actress by the Academy of Canadian Cinema and Television.

Set in London in the early 1960s, *An Education* follows Jenny, a sixteen-year-old girl, played by Carey Mulligan, as she is enticed into an affair with a much older man, portrayed by Peter Sarsgaard. Based on a memoir by Lynn Barber and adapted for the screen by Nick Hornby, the film was a critical smash. Kenneth Turan wrote for the *Los Angeles Times* (9 Oct. 2009), "*An Education* does so many things so well, it's difficult to know where to begin when cataloging its virtues." Regarding Pike's contributions, a writer for the *Scotsman* enthused, "Not only does [*An Education*] prove what a consummate scene-stealer she is, but it shows us a side of her we have never seen before: the comedienne par excellence." As an ensemble, the cast of *An Education* was nominated for a 2010 Screen Actors Guild (SAG) Award.

In March 2009, Pike played the lead in a London stage production of *Madame de Sade*. The role reunited Pike with her *Die Another Day* costar Judi Dench. Among Pike's other notable credits of 2009 is the film *Surrogates*, described by Robert Abele for the *Los Angeles Times* (25 Sep. 2009) as "a slick sci-fi number that presents a future in which flawless, hot-bodied, chicly dressed synthetic humans do the everyday living/working/playing, their every action neurally controlled by their real-human counterparts, a risk-averse population of shut-ins who've gone to seed." *Surrogates* starred Bruce Willis as a spiritually broken police officer unable to recover from the loss of his son and featured Pike as his surrogate-dependent wife.

RECENT WORK

In 2010, Pike took turns on both the stage and screen headlining a production of *Hedda Gabler*; costarring with Paul Giamatti and Dustin Hoffman in *Barney's Version*, a film adaptation of the Mordecai Richler novel; and playing a supporting role in *Made in Dagenham*, a British film about a 1968 strike by female employees at a Ford plant over gender-based pay discrimination. In each effort, Pike garnered superlative reviews. Regarding her portrayal of Hedda Gabler, Lyn Gardner wrote for the *Guardian* (7 Mar. 2010), "It is often suggested that the role of Hedda Gabler is for actresses what Hamlet is for male actors, and I've seldom seen one quite so mad, bad and dangerous to know as the Hedda offered here by Rosamund Pike. She is genuinely thrilling and genuinely scary, fixing everyone with her icy, merciless gaze, before finally turning that fatal gaze upon herself." As Miriam, the romantic obsession of Paul Giamatti's Barney in *Barney's Version*, "Pike breathes welcome warmth and life into Miriam, a paragon of wisdom, self-possession and inaccessible sex appeal," Ann Hornaday wrote. In *Made in Dagenham*, the character of Rita O'Grady, played by Sally Hawkins, leads the striking women, and as Justin Change commented for *Variety Reviews* (11 Sep. 2010), "Pike, as an upper-crust housewife sympathetic to Rita's cause, nearly upstages Hawkins in their moving scenes together."

The years 2011 and 2012 were especially busy ones for Pike. She performed in the British television miniseries *Women in Love* (2011), which was based on two D. H. Lawrence books—*The Rainbow* (1915) and *Women in Love* (1920); the Rowan Atkinson spoof of James Bond movies, *Johnny English Reborn* (2011); and the bird-watching comedy *The Big Year* (2011), starring Steve Martin, Owen Wilson, and Jack Black. She also landed a supporting role in the thriller *The Devil You Know* (2012) and played the goddess Andromeda in the blockbuster sequel *Wrath of the Titans*. She also acted alongside screen legends Tom Cruise and Robert Duvall in *Jack Reacher*, which is scheduled to open in early 2013.

Despite the increasing film and television work, Pike remains committed to the stage and has spoken of wanting to do a play every year—even with the comparatively lower pay. "My agents look on in horror, because it doesn't bring any money in at all," Pike observed to a writer for the *Scotsman*. "But I never thought I'd make any money at all doing this business. Film was never even on the cards."

PERSONAL LIFE

In the spring of 2012, Pike gave birth to her first child, a son whom she and her partner, businessman Robie Uniacke, named Solo. Pike has been with Uniacke since

December 2009, and previously she was romantically linked to actor Simon Woods and director Joe Wright, who helmed *Pride and Prejudice*.

As for her future as an actor, Pike told Lynn Barber, "I want to be respected, so that to have my name attached to a project means something. Obviously it would be great to do some wonderful enriching roles, but I want to just carry on doing it all my life. Because it just keeps you so young, it keeps you so fulfilled—it's the most fulfilling job in the world, really."

SUGGESTED READING

Barber, Lynn. "I Don't Sleep Around, If That's What You Mean . . . Would You Like Some More Cake?" *Observer*. Guardian News and Media Ltd., 23 May 2009. Web. 12 July 2012.

Cavendish, Lucy. "Rosamund Pike Interview." *Telegraph*. Telegraph Media Group Ltd., 18 Mar. 2009. Web. 12 July 2012.

Hornaday, Ann. "Rosamund Pike Talks About 'Barney's Version' and Inching into the Spotlight." *Washington Post*. The Washington Post Co., 28 Jan. 2011. Web. 12 July 2012.

Husband, Stuart. "The Name's Pike, Rosamund Pike." *Observer*. Guardian News and Media Ltd., 12 Oct. 2002. Web. 12 July 2012.

"Interview: Actress Rosamund Pike." *Scotsman.com*. Johnson Publishing Ltd., 2 Oct. 2009. Web. 12 July 2012.

Vankin, Deborah. "Rosamund Pike Isn't Afraid to Mix It Up." *Los Angeles Times*. Los Angeles Times, 2 Dec. 2010. Web. 12 July 2012.

—*Paul McCaffrey*

Andy Reid

Born: March 19, 1958
Occupation: Football coach with the Philadelphia Eagles

Philadelphia Eagles head coach and executive vice president of football operations Andy Reid has developed a reputation as one of the most admired and respected figures in the National Football League (NFL). Known for his even-tempered demeanor, meticulous organizational skills, and expert handling of players and coaches, Reid has achieved many distinctions and accolades since taking over as head coach of the Eagles in January 1999. Reid, a former offensive lineman who broke into the coaching profession as an assistant under such coaching legends as LaVell Edwards and Mike Holmgren, is the longest-tenured coach in the NFL and second-longest-tenured coach or manager in Philadelphia's professional sports history, behind Philadelphia Athletics manager Connie Mack.

Reid has also been the guiding force behind the most successful period in Eagles franchise history. Between 1999 and 2011, he led the team to six National Football Conference (NFC) East Division titles (2001–4, 2006, and 2010), five NFC Championship games (2001–4, 2008), one Super Bowl berth (2004), and 136 wins (including playoffs)—the most wins for a coach in franchise history, second only to the New England Patriots' three-time Super Bowl–winning coach Bill Belichick for most in the league since 1999. He also has the most playoff wins (10) and the highest winning percentage (.609) of any Eagles coach and is one of only five active NFL coaches with at least 100 wins. Reid's achievements have helped him earn NFL Coach of the Year honors on three occasions (2000, 2002, and 2010).

Getty Images

In addition to serving as head coach, Reid has also held the title of executive vice president of football operations with the Eagles since 2001, making him one of only a handful of NFL head coaches with the power of general manager and full autonomy over player personnel decisions. The Eagles' owner and chairman, Jeffrey Lurie, has described Reid as being "like a CEO on the field. He understands the big picture and the short-term picture. You have to always balance the two. Disciplined. Prepared. Smart. It's an awfully good combination."

EARLY LIFE

The younger of the two sons of Walter and Elizabeth Reid, Andrew Walter Reid was born on March 19, 1958, in Los Angeles, California. He and his older brother, Reginald, were raised in a two-bedroom Spanish-style home in the Los Angeles neighborhood of Los Feliz, an affluent enclave known for its many celebrity inhabitants and cultural diversity. At an early age Reid learned the importance of a strong work ethic and education from his parents, who both hailed from the East Coast. His father was an artist who designed backdrops for theatrical productions and movie sets; his mother worked as a radiologist at a hospital in the nearby city of Burbank. Reid inherited his meticulous nature from his father, who often brought him along to sets and taught him how to make cabinets and other pieces of furniture. Meanwhile, he learned organizational skills and developed a love of sports from his mother, a diehard fan of the hometown Los Angeles Dodgers, which had moved from Brooklyn, New York, to Los Angeles the year Reid was born.

Like his mother, Reid rooted for the Dodgers and regularly attended games at Dodger Stadium, which opened in 1962 and was located less than ten minutes away from his home. He was also a fan of Los Angeles's NFL team, the Rams (which later moved to St. Louis), and grew up idolizing such Rams stars as defensive tackle Merlin Olsen and defensive end Deacon Jones. Reid began playing on youth-league sports teams as a boy and spent hours each day playing football and other sports with his older brother and other neighborhood children. He has cited his brother, then a distinguished athlete at John Marshall High School in Los Angeles, as his main athletic inspiration. Physically bigger than many of his peers, Reid held his own in street pick-up games with his brother and his friends, despite the ten-year age gap between them. He later said to Jeff McLane for the *Philadelphia Inquirer* (18 June 2012), "He and his buddies made sure I wasn't going to be the big, soft kid."

Reid's large size was evident in 1971, when, at thirteen years old, he won a nationally televised NFL Punt, Pass, and Kick competition against his much smaller peers. Like his older brother, he attended John Marshall High School, where he lettered in football, basketball, baseball, and track. Despite weighing in excess of 220 pounds as a freshman, Reid proved to be a nimble athlete and became a standout offensive and defensive lineman, kicker, and punter on the school's varsity football team. As a senior cocaptain, he kicked three game-winning field goals, leading John Marshall to a 7–3 record and a berth in the quarterfinal round of the city playoffs. That year he was voted the team's most inspirational player. John Marshall High has since honored Reid with a trophy named after him, the Andy Reid Trophy, which is awarded annually to the best lineman on the football team.

EDUCATION

Reid, who was also a star pitcher and an academic standout, was offered scholarships by a number of colleges, including the University of California, Los Angeles, but turned them down in hopes of fulfilling his dream of playing for the University of Southern California (USC). After being deemed unready to play there, Reid was advised by USC's coaching staff to enroll at Glendale Community College in Glendale, California, where he played for two seasons as a starting offensive lineman and kicker. There, he developed into a Division I-A–caliber player under head coach Jim Sartoris, a former USC All-American, and was named an honorable mention All-American as a sophomore.

Prior to his junior season, Reid transferred to Brigham Young University (BYU) in Provo, Utah, which competes in the National Collegiate Athletic Association (NCAA) Football Bowl Subdivision (previously Division I-A), the highest level of college football. Reid played as an offensive lineman under legendary BYU head coach LaVell Edwards, who would become his mentor. He sat out his first year at the school to recover from a serious knee injury, suffered in the final game of his sophomore season, then spent the remainder of his career there as a backup to All-American tackle Nick Eyre. During his time at BYU, Reid wrote a sports column for the Provo *Daily Herald* that was modeled after the writing style of the late, famed *Los Angeles Times* sportswriter Jim Murray.

He also got married and converted to his wife's Mormon faith. He received a bachelor's degree in physical education from BYU in 1981.

EARLY CAREER

Though Reid had aspired to become a doctor after college, he decided instead to pursue a coaching career on the recommendation of Edwards, who believed he had a natural gift for it. He was subsequently hired by Edwards to work as a graduate assistant on BYU's coaching staff for the 1982 season. Edwards told Doug Robinson for the Salt Lake City, Utah, *Deseret Morning News* (5 Feb. 2005) that it was Reid's "temperament and his understanding of the game and his ability to work with people" that had convinced him he would make a good coach, adding, "He was a popular guy on the team, and he was a good student."

While working as a graduate assistant under Edwards at BYU, Reid met Mike Holmgren, then the school's quarterbacks coach. Impressed with Reid's strong work ethic and insatiable willingness to learn, Holmgren promised that if he ever landed an NFL head coaching job, he would hire Reid. During this time Reid began keeping daily detailed notes of his thoughts, experiences, and observations, a practice he would continue throughout his coaching career. He earned a master's degree in professional leadership in physical education and athletics from BYU in 1982.

In 1983 Reid, with the help of Edwards, landed a position as offensive coordinator at Division II San Francisco State University (SF State) in California, where he worked under renowned coach Vic Rowen. The position came with only a modest salary, so Reid took on multiple side jobs to make ends meet for his family. Those jobs included umpiring baseball games, teaching tennis and racquetball, and working as a limousine driver for such movie stars as Rock Hudson and Loni Anderson. He also sold hot dogs on SF State's campus twice a week to help raise funds for the school's cash-starved football program.

Financial struggles notwithstanding, during Reid's three-year tenure as offensive coordinator, SF State led the nation in both passing and total offense all three years. In 1986, Reid left SF State to become the offensive line coach at Northern Arizona University in Flagstaff, where he stayed for just one season. He then spent two seasons as offensive line coach at the University of Texas at El Paso, where he worked under coach Bob Stull. In 1989, he followed Stull to the University of Missouri in Columbia, where he served as offensive line coach for three seasons.

RISE TO THE NFL

When Mike Holmgren became head coach of the Green Bay Packers in 1992, Reid, as promised, was hired as the Packers' tight ends and assistant offensive line coach. Despite having little experience working with tight ends, Reid quickly picked up his new role, which helped him gain a better all-around grasp of the offense. He coached the Packers' tight ends and assisted with the offensive line for five seasons, during which he helped guide tight ends Keith Jackson and Mark Chmura to multiple Pro Bowl selections. The Packers posted winning seasons every year during that span, earning four consecutive playoff berths (1993–96) and two NFC Central Division titles (1995–96) and defeating the New England Patriots in Super Bowl XXXI, the franchise's third Super Bowl title and first since 1967.

Reid became known for putting in marathon work hours, often arriving at his office as early as three in the morning after getting just a couple hours of sleep. He would, however, return home each morning to eat breakfast and share a prayer with his family before going back to the office. He explained to Bob Ford for the *Philadelphia Inquirer* (24 Jan. 1999), "My family, my church, and my profession are the things I try to balance the best way I can. You have to have some priorities and know your life, or you spread yourself too thin. I'm constantly working at that."

After the Packers' Super Bowl–winning 1996 season, Holmgren promoted Reid to quarterbacks coach, a role he held for two seasons. In his new position Reid worked closely with Packers All-Pro quarterback Brett Favre and helped guide him to a third consecutive Associated Press (AP) NFL Most Valuable Player (MVP) Award during the 1997 season. That year the Packers finished with a 13–3 record and won a third consecutive NFC Central Division title. They advanced to the Super Bowl for the second year in a row but failed to defend their title, losing to the Denver Broncos in Super Bowl XXXII. The Packers would return to the playoffs for a sixth consecutive year in 1998, when they finished second in the NFC Central Division with a record of 11–5; however, they then lost to the San Francisco 49ers in the first round of the playoffs.

Shortly after that loss Holmgren resigned from the Packers to become head coach and general manager of the Seattle Seahawks. Under Reid's watch Favre finished the 1998 season as the NFL leader in completions, completion percentage, and passing yards. Favre described Reid to Paul Attner for *Sporting News* (23 Dec. 2002) as "a good guy, a good person," with "an ability to read players, to get them to follow him and play for him. They want to win for him; it's as simple as that."

MOVE TO PHILADELPHIA

On January 11, 1999, Reid became the twentieth head coach of the Philadelphia Eagles, hired to replace Ray Rhodes after the Eagles finished with a franchise- and league-worst 3–13 record in 1998. Reid was chosen over a number of other, more experienced candidates, many of whom had already served customary tenures as NFL offensive or defensive coordinators at the very least. In the process Reid became only the second position coach in ten years to go directly to a head-coaching job.

Despite Reid being a relatively unknown name around the league at the time and having no head-coaching experience at any level, Eagles executives were immediately blown away by his enthusiasm, intellect, and thorough preparation—he arrived at his interview with a thick binder containing detailed notes on everything from his coaching philosophies and schemes to practice and meeting schedules and even players' dress codes. Recalling his and his colleagues' first impression of Reid, Eagles owner and chairman Jeffrey Lurie told Doug Robinson, "We all looked at each other and said, 'Wow.' This guy really comes right out at you. . . . I remember how the 49ers picked Bill Walsh and the Redskins picked Joe Gibbs—out of the box." Lurie's "out of the box" hiring of Reid perplexed Philadelphia's sports media and angered much of the city's notoriously ruthless fan base, who had been expecting a more accomplished name to fill the role. Nonetheless, the risky move would prove to be one of the most rewarding of his career. Reid, who outlined his plans for rebuilding the Eagles franchise in his first news conference, was signed to a five-year deal worth approximately $5 million.

Reid's tenure with the Eagles got off to a rocky start. In one of his first major moves at the helm, he used the second overall pick in the 1999 NFL Draft to select quarterback Donovan McNabb, a choice that was famously met with a chorus of boos by Eagles fans on draft day. Though McNabb had amassed a decorated All-American career at Syracuse University, many fans—including Philadelphia's then mayor, former Pennsylvania governor Edward G. Rendell—had lobbied hard for the Eagles to draft Heisman Trophy–winning running back Ricky Williams of the University of Texas. Fans and critics became more incensed when the Eagles began the 1999 season by losing seven of their first nine games, while Reid kept McNabb on the bench to develop under veteran quarterback Doug Pederson. Although McNabb went on to start the last seven games of that season, the Eagles finished last in the NFC East Division for the second consecutive year, with a record of 5–11.

MASTER PLAN

Eagles fans saw the first glimpses of Reid's master plan for the franchise during the 2000 season, when he led the team to an 11–5 record and a second-place finish in NFC East Division, marking the greatest single-season turnaround in franchise history. That year saw McNabb emerge as the star franchise quarterback that Reid had originally envisioned he would become, as he accounted for nearly 75 percent of the Eagles' total offense, setting new team records for passing attempts and completions and leading all NFL quarterbacks with a career-high 629 rushing yards. He subsequently earned his first career Pro Bowl selection and finished second in the voting for the AP NFL MVP Award, beaten only by St. Louis Rams running back Marshall Faulk. On the strength of McNabb's play, the Eagles earned their first playoff berth since 1996 and advanced to the NFC divisional playoff round, where they lost to the New York Giants. The team's remarkable turnaround helped Reid earn NFL Coach of the Year honors from the Maxwell Football Club, *Football Digest*, and *Sporting News*.

Over the next four seasons, Reid would transform "the most cynical and frustrated of sports cities and teams from a perennial loser into a perennial contender," as Doug Robinson noted. The Eagles posted records of 11–5, 12–4, 12–4, and 13–3 from 2001 to 2004, winning four consecutive NFC East titles and advancing to four straight NFC Championship games. In 2002 Reid was named the AP NFL Coach of the Year and the Maxwell Football Club NFL Coach of the Year, having helped the Eagles tie for the best record in the league despite losing McNabb for the last six games of the season due to a broken ankle. The following season, Reid led the

Eagles to the top record in the NFC for the second straight year, with the team winning twelve of their last fourteen games.

The Eagles carried that momentum into the 2004 season, winning thirteen of their first fourteen games and finishing with the number-one seed in the NFL playoffs. They would subsequently put behind them the agony of three straight defeats in the previous three NFC title games by defeating the Atlanta Falcons in the 2004 NFC Championship Game and advancing to the franchise's first Super Bowl since 1980. In Super Bowl XXXIX, the Eagles lost to the defending champion, the New England Patriots, in a dramatic game that was not determined until the final minutes. Despite the loss, Reid ended that season with seventy-one career wins—the most of any coach in Eagles history, surpassing Hall of Famer Earle "Greasy" Neale's previous record of sixty-six career wins with the club.

LATER SEASONS

Following a disappointing 2005 season in which the Eagles failed to qualify for the playoffs, Reid helped the team return to form in 2006 with their fifth NFC East title in six seasons. Despite sputtering to a 5–6 start and playing the last six games of the season without McNabb, who had gone down with a season-ending injury for the second consecutive year, the Eagles rattled off five consecutive wins to end the year under backup quarterback Jeff Garcia. They went on to defeat their NFC East rival, the New York Giants, in the NFC wild-card round of the playoffs before losing to the New Orleans Saints in the NFC divisional round.

Shortly after that loss, Reid took a five-week leave from the Eagles to tend to legal matters involving his two eldest sons, Garrett and Britt, both of whom were arrested on gun- and drug-related charges in separate incidents on January 30, 2007. He accompanied both of his sons to a rehabilitation facility in Florida. The two were later ordered to serve short prison sentences for their crimes.

After dealing with his family crisis, Reid returned to the Eagles for the 2007 season, hoping to build on his team's success from the previous year. The team, however, struggled to an 8–8 record and finished in last place in the NFC East. The Eagles bounced back and reestablished themselves among the NFL's elite in 2008, finishing second in the NFC East with a 9–6–1 record and advancing to their fifth NFC Championship game in eight seasons, where they lost to the Arizona Cardinals. That season Reid became the thirty-seventh coach in NFL history to reach one hundred career wins and only the twenty-second to accomplish the feat with a single franchise.

> "My family, my church, and my profession are the things I try to balance the best way I can. You have to have some priorities and know your life, or you spread yourself too thin. I'm constantly working at that."

Reid led the Eagles back to the playoffs in 2009 and 2010, where they finished second and first in the NFC East, with records of 11–5 and 10–6, respectively. In

2010, he also coached reborn quarterback Michael Vick, who had joined the team the previous year in a backup role after serving nearly two years in prison for running an illegal intrastate dogfighting ring, to a surprising Pro Bowl campaign, with Vick leading an explosive Eagles offense that finished second in the NFL in total offense. Though the Eagles lost to the eventual Super Bowl champion Green Bay Packers in the wild-card playoff round, Reid was named the Maxwell Football Club NFL Coach of the Year for the third time in his career, while Vick was named the NFL Comeback Player of the Year.

After making several notable free-agent acquisitions during the 2011 off-season, Reid's Eagles entered the 2011 season as legitimate Super Bowl contenders. They ultimately failed to live up to expectations, however, finishing second in the NFC East with an 8–8 record and missing the playoffs for the first time since 2007. The team entered the 2012 season with similar aspirations, and Reid came into the season with the second-highest winning percentage among active NFL coaches with at least one hundred games to their credit.

Reid is one of thirty-one coaches in NFL history to have coached two hundred or more regular-season games and is only the thirteenth to do so with one team. He is also one of just eleven coaches in league history to remain with his original team for twelve or more seasons. Reid has developed more first-time Pro Bowl players (nineteen) than any other coach in the league since becoming the Eagles' coach in 1999, and, like his mentor Mike Holmgren, he has overseen a number of assistants who have gone on to NFL head coaching careers, among them Baltimore Ravens coach John Harbaugh, Minnesota Vikings coach Leslie Frazier, Carolina Panthers coach Ron Rivera, and Cleveland Browns coach Pat Shurmur. Reid is signed with the Eagles through the 2013 season.

PERSONAL LIFE

Reid and his wife, Tammy, live in the affluent Philadelphia suburb of Villanova. They are devout Mormon and members of the Church of Jesus Christ of Latter-Day Saints. As part of his Mormon faith, Reid abstains from drinking alcohol, smoking, and swearing. He was inducted into the Glendale Community College Athletic Hall of Fame in 2003 and into the John Marshall Athletic Hall of Fame in 2012.

On August 5, 2012, Reid's eldest son, Garrett, was found dead in his dorm room at Lehigh University, where he had been working as an assistant to the Eagles' strength and conditioning coaches during the team's annual NFL training camp. While no official cause of death was released, Reid hinted in a statement to the media that his son's death may have been drug related. Among the more than nine hundred people who attended Garrett Reid's funeral were the entire Eagles organization, NFL commissioner Roger Goodell, Patriots coach Bill Belichick, Holmgren, Harbaugh, and numerous other current and former players, coaches, and officials. In the Eagles' 2012 preseason opener, Eagles players honored Garrett by wearing black helmet decals emblazoned with his initials.

Reid and his wife have two other sons, Britt and Spencer, and two daughters, Crosby and Drew Ann.

SUGGESTED READING

Attner, Paul. "A Bear of a Man, a Winner of a Plan." *Sporting News* 23 Dec. 2002: 22–25. Print.

Bowen, Les. *Philadelphia Eagles: The Complete Illustrated History.* Minneapolis: MVP, 2011. Print.

Didinger, Ray, and Robert S. Lyons. *The Eagles Encyclopedia.* Philadelphia: Temple UP, 2005. Print.

Ford, Bob. "The Eagles' New Coach Is the Man with the Plan." *Philly.com.* Philadelphia Media Network, 24 Jan. 1999. Web. 16 Aug. 2012.

Harmon, Dick. "Count on This: Reid Will Have Eagles Prepared." *HeraldExtra.com.* Daily Herald, 27 Jan. 2002. Web. 16 Aug. 2012.

McLane, Jeff. "Back to Coach Reid's Old Stomping Ground." *Philly.com.* Philadelphia Media Network, 18 June 2012. Web. 16 Aug. 2012.

Robinson, Doug. "Reid Soars: Eagles Coach Studied at Foot of LaVell Edwards." *DeseretNews.com.* Deseret News, 5 Feb. 2005. Web. 16 Aug. 2012.

—*Chris Cullen*

Manon Rhéaume

Born: February 24, 1972
Occupation: Hockey player

Manon Rhéaume was thrust into the spotlight in September 1992, when she received an invitation to attend training camp for the National Hockey League (NHL) team Tampa Bay Lightning. Although Phil Esposito, the Lightning's president and general manager, conceded that the invitation was a publicity stunt, Rhéaume capitalized on the opportunity. "When I started playing hockey I was the only girl and, often, I wasn't chosen for the top teams because I was a girl," she told Kristen Odland for the *Calgary Herald* (24 Jan. 2009). "Here and there, I [was] fortunate people didn't let that stop them from choosing me

Getty Images

. . . they just wanted the best goaltender. . . . So, when I got invited to Tampa Bay—at that point, I didn't care why they invited me. I had an opportunity to play at the highest level possible. I didn't want to have any regrets." Rhéaume's appearance during an exhibition game marked the first time that a woman had played in a men's professional hockey league, thus elevating her to pioneer status. She has since played for various men's hockey teams, most recently the Flint Generals.

EARLY LIFE

Manon Rhéaume was born on February 24, 1972, to Nicole and Pierre Rhéaume in the tiny ski-resort town of Lac-Beauport, a suburb of Quebec City, Quebec. She is the middle of three children, with an older brother, Martin, and a younger one named Pascal. She first learned to skate as a three-year-old and started donning goalie pads at the age of five, after being introduced to the sport of ice hockey by her father, a contractor who managed the town's outdoor skating rink and also served as the coach of his sons' novice hockey team. Rhéaume would wear padded clothing and block shots during practice sessions in her family's backyard rink. "My mom thought I was crazy," she told Mark Johnson for the Milwaukee *Journal Sentinel* (8 Aug. 2005) "At the time, nobody was playing hockey if you were a girl."

At age five, Rhéaume made her competitive debut, patrolling the net for her brothers' team at a tournament. "I said to my father, 'I would like to be your goaltender.' He laughed. But then he said, 'Why not? You take shots from your brothers at home,'" she recalled to William Plummer for *People* (28 Sep. 1992). Growing up, Rhéaume often competed against boys while playing youth hockey in the Quebec City area. "Manon was always too strong for the girls," her mother told Christopher Sullivan for the Associated Press (22 Nov. 1992).

However, Rhéaume, who also participated in other sports for a time, including ballet, baseball, and skiing, faced discrimination and some backlash for playing on all-boys' teams. "So many parents think their boy should go into the National Hockey League," she said to Linda Kay for the *Chicago Tribune* (16 Dec. 1991). "When I would try out for a spot as a goalie, some parents thought I was taking a position that should have gone to their boy."

YOUTH PIONEER

The eleven-year-old Rhéaume made history in 1984, when she became the first girl ever to take part in the world's largest and most prestigious international youth-hockey event: the Quebec International Pee-Wee Hockey Tournament, an annual eleven-day competition held each February in Quebec City. By the age of twelve, Rhéaume was playing pee-wee hockey on a year-round basis. "It was my passion," she told Plummer. Rhéaume achieved another milestone by becoming the first girl to play in the bantam division (for ages thirteen and fourteen) at the double-A level, also known as tier-two hockey, which is regarded as youth hockey's second-highest competitive skill level.

However, Rhéaume became discouraged when she was not given the opportunity to try out for any tier-one teams in the midget division (ages fifteen to seventeen), a step below the junior hockey level, the top players of which are recruited into the professional ranks. When she turned seventeen years old, she took a hiatus from her favorite sport and focused instead on her studies, enrolling at a junior college in Sainte-Foy, now part of Quebec City. However, after her first year of school, the eighteen-year-old Rhéaume resumed playing hockey and joined a women's team in Sherbrooke. In 1991, the competitive squad won a regional tournament to advance to the Esso Women's Nationals, where Rhéaume's team lost in the finals to the North York Aeros of Ontario.

Following the end of the 1991 season, Rhéaume received a surprise invitation to attend training camp with the Louisville Jaguars, an all-men's junior ice-hockey squad whose roster also included her younger brother, Pascal. (Founded in 1990 as the Saint-Antoine Rapidos, the Jaguars—since renamed the Saint-Jérôme Panthers—were at the time a farm team of the Trois-Rivières Draveurs, who competed in the Quebec Major Junior Hockey League, one of the three leagues that comprise the Canadian Hockey League.) Rhéaume beat out four other male candidates for the backup goalie position on the tier-two team.

In late November 1991 she received a call-up to the Draveurs squad due to an injury sustained by the starting goaltender. Rhéaume, who served as the backup to second-string goalie Jocelyn Thibault, made her debut against the Granby Bisons. Rhéaume made history with her appearance, becoming the first female goalie to play in the Quebec Major Junior Hockey League and the first female player to appear in a men's top-level hockey game. She played for seventeen minutes, allowing three goals, and was removed from the game after a puck hit her protective mask, leaving a gash over her right eye; the wound would later require stitches.

GOLD MEDAL FOR TEAM CANADA

In 1992, Rhéaume was named a member of the Canadian national women's hockey squad. She competed in the International Ice Hockey Federation (IIHF) World Women's Championships, a prestigious international women's tournament that was held in April in Tampere, Finland. The Canadian team dominated the first-round competition, defeating China, Denmark, and Sweden to advance to the final round. After a decisive four-run semifinal victory over Finland, Team Canada defeated the US in the finals, scoring eight unanswered goals. During her team's dominating performance, Rhéaume earned three wins, including two shutouts, and only allowed two goals. She was named to the tournament's all-star squad.

TURNING PROFESSIONAL

In August 1992, Rhéaume accepted an invitation to training camp from the Tampa Bay Lightning. In doing so, she became not only the first woman to try out for a club in the National Hockey League (NHL) but also the first to sign a professional hockey deal. On September 23, 1992, Rhéaume achieved another milestone by becoming the first woman to play in an NHL exhibition game. She played for one period and allowed two goals while blocking seven of nine shots during a preseason loss to the St. Louis Blues. In the wake of her achievement, Rhéaume became an international phenomenon, appearing on several high-profile television shows, including Late Night with David Letterman, The Today Show, and Entertainment Tonight.

In November, after failing to make the team out of training camp, Rhéaume signed a three-year contract with the Atlanta Knights, Tampa Bay's top minor-league squad in the International Hockey League (IHL). On December 13, 1992, she became the first woman to play a regular-season game in the IHL. Rhéaume, who replaced starter David Littman during the second period, played for five minutes; she blocked three shots and gave up only one goal against the Salt Lake Golden Eagles, who won 4–1.

Rhéaume made headlines again on April 10, 1993, when she made her first start in goal for the Knights in front of a home crowd of twenty thousand people. The appearance marked the first time that a woman had started a regular-season professional hockey game. Although Rhéaume had twenty-five blocked shots, she allowed six goals to the visiting Cincinnati Cyclones before being removed during the third period for an extra skater. The Cyclones scored two more empty net goals to win 8–6.

Rhéaume's next appearance for the Knights came during a preseason game against the Boston Bruins in October 1993. Following a poor performance at the start of the 1993–94 regular season, during which Rhéaume surrendered three first-period goals en route to a 4–2 loss, the Knights demoted her to the now-defunct Knoxville Cherokees of the East Coast Hockey League (ECHL), another Tampa Bay Lightning affiliate. On November 6, 1993, Rhéaume, the third-string goalie, was designated to start against the Johnstown Chiefs. She played the entire game, blocking thirty-two out of thirty-eight

> *"So, when I got invited to Tampa Bay—at that point, I didn't care why they invited me. I had an opportunity to play at the highest level possible. I didn't want to have any regrets."*

shots for a 9–6 victory. This achievement earned Rhéaume the distinction of being the second female goalie to start and win a professional hockey game; Erin Whitten of the Toledo Storm was the first.

In February 26, 1994, Rhéaume, who had recorded another victory and a tie in three more games with the Cherokees, was traded to the Nashville Knights, a former affiliate of the Tampa Bay Lightning. As a member of the Nashville Knights (1993–94), she recorded three wins in four games while making 109 saves and surrendering twelve goals.

WINNING MORE MEDALS

In April 1994, Rhéaume was part of the Canadian women's national hockey team that traveled to Lake Placid, New York, to defend its 1992 gold medal at the IIHF Women's World Championships. Team Canada advanced to the final round of the tournament, following first-round victories against China, Norway, and Sweden.

After defeating Finland in the semifinals, the Canadian squad faced off against Team USA in a finals rematch and captured their second consecutive IIHF World Championship gold medal. Rhéaume compiled a record of three wins in four games, with six goals allowed, during Team Canada's gold-medal run. For the second time in her career, she was voted to the tournament's all-star team.

During the summer Rhéaume played for the New Jersey Rockin Rollers, a squad that competed in Roller Hockey International (RHI), a now-defunct men's inline-hockey league. By November of that year, Rhéaume had returned to the IHL after a trade from the Nashville Knights to the Las Vegas Thunder; in 1994–95 she blocked fourteen shots and allowed three goals in two games. Following her brief stint with the Thunder, Rhéaume spent 1994–95 with another Las Vegas–based team: the Aces, a semiprofessional squad in the Pacific Southwest Hockey League (PSHL). That same season she also suited up for the Tallahassee Tiger Sharks of the ECHL, giving up four goals and making twelve saves in her only appearance with the team. Rhéaume continued to garner attention in 1995, when she appeared in an exhibition match, also known as a friendly game, with VEU Feldkirch, an Austrian men's ice-hockey club.

Between 1995 and 1997, Rhéaume played for two professional roller-hockey teams in the RHI, the Ottawa Loggers and the Sacramento River Rats. In October 1996, she traveled with the women's national hockey team to compete at the Pacific Rim Three Nations Cup, where Team Canada reached the finals against perennial rivals Team USA. Following her team's shutout victory, Rhéaume added another gold medal to her record. A month later, she signed a deal with the Nevada-based Reno Renegades, a now-defunct minor-league ice-hockey squad in the West Coast Hockey League (WCHL). During the 1996–97 regular season, Rhéaume appeared in eleven games, making 262 saves and allowing forty goals while amassing a record of two wins, three losses, and a tie.

In the summer of 1998, the first year that women's hockey made its Olympic debut, Rhéaume rejoined the national hockey squad for the Winter Games in Nagano, Japan. Team Canada, the gold-medal favorites, advanced to the medal round after compiling a first-round record of four wins and one loss to finish second behind the undefeated Team USA. The two teams went head-to-head in the finals, where the American squad finally triumphed over Rhéaume and her compatriots to claim the gold medal.

BLAZING NEW TRAILS

After winning silver at the 1998 Olympic Games, Rhéaume took a sabbatical from playing hockey in 1998. She spent the 1999–2000 season serving as goaltending coach for the University of Minnesota-Duluth (UMD) Bulldogs, the women's ice-hockey team. In 1999, Rhéaume was not selected to be part of the Canadian women's hockey team that captured gold at the 2000 IIHF World Women's Championships, hosted that year in Canada. She officially announced her decision to retire from international competition in July 2000, following an eight-year stint as the goaltender for the Canadian national women's squad.

In search of a new challenge, Rhéaume signed a contract in September 2000 to play forward for the Montreal Wingstars in the National Women's Hockey League (NWHL). After ending the 2000–2001 season with a record of thirty wins, six losses, and four ties to finish first in the Eastern Division, the Wingstars were eliminated in the first round of the playoffs by their division rivals, the Sainte-Julie Pantheres.

While playing for the Wingstars, Rhéaume was hired by Mission Hockey, an athletic equipment manufacturer in Irvine, California. As the company's head of global marketing, she spent three years helping to create and market the Betty Flyweight, a brand of skates specifically designed for women. In 2003 Rhéaume started working as the director of marketing and coordinator of girls' hockey programs at the Powerade Iceport, a five-rink sports facility in Cudahy, Wisconsin. Two years later, she accepted a position in Farmington Hills, Michigan, as the director of marketing and sales at the Central Collegiate Hockey Association (CCHA), one of the country's premier men's hockey conferences.

Rhéaume was a member of the Little Caesars senior women's amateur squad that won the 2008 USA Hockey Women's Senior A National Championships in West Chester, Pennsylvania. That same year she created an eponymous foundation with the goal of granting scholarships to young female athletes. She also sought to kick start her playing career by attending the training camp of the Port Huron Icehawks, a Michigan-based minor-league team in the IHL. In 2009 Rhéaume was signed by the Minnesota Whitecaps of the Western Women's Hockey League (WWHL). She was the goaltender for the team, which reached the finals of the inaugural 2009 Clarkson Cup before losing to the Montreal Stars. Rhéaume made headlines again in April of that year when she played for the Flint Generals of the IHL, becoming the third woman to suit up for the men's team.

PERSONAL LIFE

Rhéaume, the founder of an eponymous international women's invitational hockey tournament, published her autobiography, *Manon: Alone in Front of the Net*, in 1993. She was also the subject of *Manon Rhéaume: Woman behind the Mask*, an hour-long documentary that aired on Canadian television in 2000. She has a son, Dylan, from her first marriage in 1998 to former hockey player Gerry St. Cyr, whom she later divorced. Since then, she has reportedly remarried and has a second son.

SUGGESTED READING

Brody, Susan. "100 Greatest Female Athletes." *Sports Illustrated Women*. CNN/ Sports Illustrated, n.d. Web. 12 July 2012.

Caputo, Pat. "When in Rhéaume: Female Youth Players Follow in Pioneer's Footsteps." *Oakland Press*. Oakland Press, 12 Nov. 2009. Web. 12 July 2012.

Dillman, Lisa. "Manon Among Boys: Professional Hockey's First Female Players Makes First Start Tonight for Minor League Team." *Los Angeles Times*. Los Angeles Times, 10 Apr. 1993. Web. 12 July 2012.

Johnson, Mark. "Female Hockey Pioneer Calls the Shots Now: Manon Rhéaume Is Coaching and Directing Girls Hockey in the Milwaukee Area." *Madison.com*. Madison.com, 8 Aug. 2005. Web. 12 July 2012.

Odland, Kristen. "Rhéaume Helped Make Hockey a Girls' Game." *Canada.com*. Postmedia Network, 24 Jan. 2009. Web. 12 July 2012.

Plummer, William. "The Puck Stops Here." *People* 28 Sep. 1992: 85–88. Print.

Shine, T. M. "Girl With A Goal: The First Woman to Try Out for a Professional Hockey Team Seems Ready, Willing, Able and Coolly Confident." *Sun Sentinel* [South Florida]. Tribune, 22 Sep. 1992. Web. 12 July 2012.

Sullivan, Christopher. "On Ice and Off, 'a Lot of Pressure, a Lot of Action.'" *Los Angeles Times*. Los Angeles Times, 22 Nov. 1992. Web. 12 July 2012.

Villiers, Kelly. "Knights Goalie Adjusting to Male Sports World." *Seattle Times*. Seattle Times, 10 Jan. 1993. Web. 12 July 2012.

—Bertha Muteba

Adam Riess

Born: December 16, 1969
Occupation: Astrophysicist, educator

"The research that leads to a Nobel Prize in physics can sometimes be a little obscure," Michael D. Lemonick wrote for *Time* magazine (5 Oct. 2011). "In 1990, for example, three scientists got the nod 'for their pioneering investigations concerning deep inelastic scattering of electrons on protons and bound neutrons.' Got that? The next year, the prize went to a scientist 'for discovering that methods developed for studying order phenomena in simple systems can be generalized to more complex forms of matter.' But sometimes, you just can't help saying, 'Wow!' and maybe: 'What took the Nobel folks so long?'" The

© The Nobel Foundation. Photo: Ulla Montan

discovery that elicited a "Wow" from Lemonick was made, in part, by Nobel laureate Adam Riess, a physicist from Johns Hopkins University. Riess and his colleagues had found that the universe, contrary to previous beliefs, was expanding faster and faster as time went on, and that the phenomenon was probably due to a mysterious force known as dark energy, which is now thought to comprise fully three-quarters of the universe.

EARLY LIFE AND EDUCATION

Adam Riess was born on December 16, 1969, in Washington, DC. His father, Michael, was a US Navy engineer who served during the 1960s as chief scientist for antisubmarine warfare. He later moved the family to Warren, New Jersey, where he owned and operated a frozen food distributorship and pursued various other entrepreneurial ventures. Riess's mother, Doris, maintained a thriving practice as a clinical psychologist. Riess's paternal grandfather was the respected journalist Curt Riess, who was best known for his reporting during World War II, as well as for such books as *The Nazis Go Underground* (1944), about Germany's efforts at espionage, and *The Berlin Story* (1952), a cultural history of that city. Adam, the youngest of Doris and Michael's children, has two older sisters: Gail Saltz, a psychiatrist and media commentator, and Holly Hagerman, an artist who specializes in oil portraits.

As a child, Riess loved sports and was particularly enamored of soccer. In addition to his physical prowess, Riess exhibited great intellectual curiosity. "Besides pestering my family with questions," he wrote in a statement posted on the Shaw Prize website, "I conducted my own 'experiments' to learn about the world around me including sticking wires into electrical outlets, tasting everything in the spice rack and cutting earthworms in half—all to see what would happen." He was exceptionally interested in dinosaurs and toyed with the idea of becoming a paleontologist one day.

Along with his sisters, who were also precocious, Riess built a tree house when he was about eight years old. The difference between the Riess children's structure and others in their suburban neighborhood, however, was that they constructed a working telegraph line for theirs. Excited about the burgeoning computer technology of the day, Riess had learned programming by the time he was eleven and was teaching an adult education course in computer use by the time he was in his teens.

Although his children were undeniably bright, Riess's father nonetheless insisted that they learn the value of physical labor, and all three were made to work at a delicatessen he once owned. On one memorable day a customer became ill in the restroom. Sent to clean the mess, Riess balked. "[My father] lit into me later about that," he recalled to Michael Anft for *Johns Hopkins Magazine* (Feb. 2008). "He told me, 'You have to do what you have to do. You think you're better than everyone else there?' He let me know that there were people who had to do that kind of work for a living. What I took from all that was that I had to really work hard to do the things I like. I was terrified of having to do something where I would just watch the clock."

Riess attended the Watchung Hills Regional High School, one of New Jersey's most highly ranked secondary schools. Designated both a National Merit Scholar and Garden State Distinguished Scholar, he served as president of the National Honor Society, and during his senior year he won prizes for outstanding performances in calculus and biology. In addition to his love of science, he maintained a deep interest in history, especially the American Civil War. He also worked on the school newspaper and was a valued member of the Watchung Hills Academic Team. When he graduated in 1988, he was named salutatorian.

Upon leaving Watchung Hills, Riess entered the Massachusetts Institute of Technology (MIT), where he majored in physics. He had maintained his love for history and chose it as his minor field of study; his final research paper, which drew upon his deep knowledge of sports, focused on the so-called Black Sox scandal of 1919. At MIT Riess was a member of Phi Delta Theta and roomed at a fraternity house overlooking the Charles River. As in high school, Riess excelled, earning a 4.94 grade point average (on a 5.0 scale) and being elected to the academic honors society Phi Beta Kappa. While at MIT he served during the summer as an intern at the Lawrence Livermore National Laboratory, a California-based government institution with a mission to use "science and technology in the national interest," particularly in regard to issues of national security. At Livermore Riess was involved in the search for Massive Compact Halo Objects (MACHOs)—bodies of matter that emit no light, such as neutron stars or red dwarf stars. In 1992 Riess graduated from MIT with a bachelor's degree and embarked on graduate studies.

A NEW CHAPTER AT HARVARD

Riess next enrolled at Harvard University, thinking that he might become involved in the search for extraterrestrial intelligence (SETI). After realizing that he might never gather enough data to support a thesis, he changed his focus. "I knew next to nothing about astronomy or astrophysics. But I was intrigued with ideas like, How will the universe end? and, How long has it been here? These were the big questions," he told Anft. "What I was amazed to find was that this wasn't just a subject for speculation. You could go out with a telescope and answer them. It may be difficult, but there's a methodology." Riess began studying under Robert Kirshner, a renowned physics professor who had earned a global reputation for his research on supernovae.

A supernova occurs when a star explodes at the end of its life, giving off an incredible burst of light that can be seen at distances of up to 10 billion light-years. This can happen in two ways. In the first case, a stars run out of fuel and cannot sustain itself against its own weight. The central part subsequently collapses, and the outer layers of the star fall in on the core and then rebound in a massive explosion. In the second set of circumstances, matter piling up on the compressed core of an already dead star reaches sufficient density to trigger the explosion. In an article for the *New York Times* (18 Feb. 2003), Dennis Overbye explained that "the exploding stars of choice are known as Type Ia. They originate on dense burned-out cinders about the size of Earth that are known to astronomers as white dwarfs." He added that "if a white dwarf has a companion star, it can have a violent, brief resurrection as a Type Ia supernova. In that case, the intense gravity of the white dwarf can steal material from its neighbor. When its mass exceeds a critical limit, about 1.4 times the mass of the sun, the star destroys itself in a fury as bright as four billion suns." The brightness of these Type Ia explosions can be used to help calculate their distance. Because they had exploded when the universe was young, the supernovae farthest away from the Earth could provide valuable information to scientists about conditions at that time.

Riess proved to be a talented graduate student. When assigned to teach undergraduates, he frequently structured his classes along the lines of a game show so that they would be encouraged to participate. He was especially adept at conveying complex concepts to laypeople; later, as a full professor at Johns Hopkins, he began regularly teaching a course dubbed Great Discoveries in Astronomy and Astrophysics, geared toward humanities majors. Working closely with Kirshner and another Harvard professor, William Press, he learned to make precise measurements with telescopes and analyze the data retrieved. His doctoral thesis, "The Multicolor Light Curve Shape Method," detailed a method by which scientists could account for the effect of variables—such as the presence of cosmic dust or differing luminosities and colors—when measuring supernovae. The paper later won him the annual Astronomical Society of the Pacific (ASP) Robert J. Trumpler Award, given for a thesis of great significance by a North American doctoral candidate. Riess earned his PhD from Harvard in 1996.

THE HIGH-Z SUPERNOVA TEAM

Upon earning his doctoral degree, Riess accepted a three-year Miller Research Fellowship from the University of California, Berkeley. He also joined the High-Z Supernova Team, a group of international scientists. High-Z is a reference to redshift (represented by a "z" in scientific equations) which is the Doppler effect observed when a celestial object is moving farther away from Earth. A few years before, Saul Perlmutter, with whom Riess would eventually share many of the science world's top honors, had begun leading a team at the Lawrence Berkeley National Laboratory to meticulously search the cosmos for supernovae. Now, Schmidt's competing team, which also included Kirshner, tapped Riess to analyze data for a project titled "Measuring the Cosmic Deceleration and Global Geometry of the Universe with Type Ia Supernovae." Although the work was sure to be painstaking and unglamorous, Riess agreed. (Somewhat ironically, his office at the university was located only a short distance from that of Perlmutter at the national lab.)

"The Universe is behaving like a driver who slows down approaching a red stoplight and then hits the accelerator when the light turns green."

Soon, both teams were collecting confusing data. The expansion of the universe that started with the big bang some thirteen million years ago had long been thought to be slowing, as the outward push of individual galaxies was affected by gravitational pull. New data, however, seemed to be showing that the expansion was instead speeding up. "The Universe is behaving like a driver who slows down approaching a red stoplight and then hits the accelerator when the light turns green," Riess explained to David Whitehouse for the BBC News (4 Apr. 2001), using one of the vivid metaphors for which he has become known. He has also compared the galaxies to raisins in a loaf of bread made with a lot of yeast, pushing vigorously away from each other as the loaf rises.

Although Riess was reassured somewhat when he found out that Perlmutter's team was attaining similar results, he still worried that he had made a mistake in his calculations. They were not the only scientists ever stymied by such an issue. "I liken it to if you took a pair of keys and threw them up in the air with the purpose of measuring how fast they fall back down, to measure how much the Earth tugs at your keys, and then they went up instead," Riess told Ira Flatow, the host of the National Public Radio program *Science Friday* (16 Mar. 2012). "You would be very confused, and that's the position my colleagues and I were in, in 1998, when we saw the universe not slowing down as we expected but actually speeding up, implying the existence of this very mysterious dark energy."

The dark energy to which he was referring was a source of much excitement in the scientific community. Physicists had long spoken of four basic forces: gravity, a strong force that holds atoms together, a weak force that keeps electrons in place, and electromagnetism. Now, suddenly, it seemed that a fifth force—dark energy—not only existed but made up the vast majority of the universe. "Dark energy is the name given to an unexplained force that is drawing galaxies away from each other, against the pull of gravity, at an accelerated pace," Clara Moskowitz wrote for Space.com (27 Apr. 2009). She added: "Dark energy is a bit like anti-gravity. Where gravity pulls things together at the more local level, dark energy tugs them apart on the grander scale." A few days after the High-Z Team announced their findings about the expansion of the universe, Perlmutter's team confirmed that they had reached the same conclusion. The editors of *Science* magazine deemed it 1998's "breakthrough of the year."

A MOVE TO BALTIMORE

Despite the accolades and excitement, Riess knew that further investigation was needed. He wanted to measure supernovae even farther away—from the era before dark energy began to exert its pull, roughly seven billion years ago. If the pace of expansion was truly accelerating, those supernovae would appear brighter than expected. The only telescope capable of helping was the powerful Hubble, and in 1999 Riess joined Baltimore's Space Telescope Science Institute, where it was housed. In 2001 Riess and his colleagues found a supernova 11 billion light-years away that was, indeed, twice as bright as expected. The Hubble telescope had recorded it two years earlier, but it had gone unnoticed until Riess reviewed the images. (He has described looking at such images as akin to viewing a television screen full of static.) Still, he continued to search for corroborating evidence, a task made easier when the Hubble was fitted with a new, more powerful camera. Within a few years Riess had measured the dozen most distant supernovae ever found, confirming his theory.

AWARDS

Riess has since received numerous prizes for his work. In 2006, the year he joined the faculty at Johns Hopkins University, he shared the prestigious Shaw Prize for Astronomy with Perlmutter and Schmidt. In 2008 he was awarded a fellowship from the John D. and Catherine T. MacArthur Foundation. The fellowship includes a $500,000 monetary award, nicknamed the Genius Grant. His biggest honor came in 2011, when he received a call from Sweden early one morning. The caller, from the Royal Swedish Academy of Sciences in Stockholm, informed him that he would be sharing that year's Nobel Prize in Physics with Perlmutter and Schmidt, for their "discovery of the accelerating expansion of the Universe through observations of distant supernovae." Perlmutter received half of the 10 million kroner prize (about $750,000), while Riess and Schmidt each received a quarter (about $325,000).

PERSONAL LIFE

Since 1998 Riess has been married to Nancy Joy Schondorf, an industrial designer whom he had met while at MIT. When Riess left for Harvard, the pair communicated by blinking flashlights across the Charles River. They have a daughter, Gabrielle, born in 2004, and a son, Noah, born in 2010. When Gabrielle was a toddler, Riess referred to her as "my favorite supernova."

Despite the sometimes cutthroat competition of the science world, Riess has been widely praised as a generous and gracious person. In his spare time he enjoys watching professional football and collecting historical coins. He has good-naturedly admitted that he cannot identify most constellations and is able to find only the Big Dipper with any degree of accuracy.

SUGGESTED READING

Anft, Michael. "Chasing the Great Beyond." *Johns Hopkins Magazine*. Johns Hopkins University, Feb. 2008. Web. 1 Mar. 2012.

Clark, Stuart. "Heart of Darkness." *New Scientist* 17 Feb. 2007: 28. Print.

Easterbrook, Gregg. "The Revolutionary Ideas of Nobelist Adam Riess." *TheAtlantic. com*. Atlantic Monthly Group, 4 Oct. 2010. Web. 1 Mar. 2012.

Lemonick, Michael D. "The Physics Nobel: Why Einstein Was Wrong About Being Wrong." *Time*. Time, 5 Oct. 2011. Web. 01 Mar. 2012.

Overbye, Dennis. "Scientist at Work: Adam Riess: His Prey: Dark Energy in the Cosmic Abyss." *New York Times* 18 Feb. 2003: F01. Print.

—Mari Rich

Aaron Rodgers

Born: December 2, 1983
Occupation: Football player with the Green Bay Packers

"I want to be the best," Green Bay Packers quarterback Aaron Rodgers told Lori Nickel for the Milwaukee *Journal Sentinel* (24 Oct. 2010). "I've always wanted to be the best." In four full seasons as the Packers' starting quarterback, Rodgers has, in fact, established himself as arguably the best quarterback in the National Football League (NFL). In reaching such elite status, however, Rodgers has had to overcome significant obstacles: He was not recruited out of high school, and despite enjoying a decorated two-year college career at the University of California, Berkeley, he was only the twenty-fourth overall selection of

Getty Images

the 2005 NFL Draft, in which he was taken by the Packers. Furthermore, he was relegated to the backup quarterback role for three years, deferring to the Packers' legendary quarterback Brett Favre.

Finally getting his chance to start during the 2008 season (when Favre, who had retired and then unretired, was traded to the New York Jets), Rodgers passed for more than four thousand yards and twenty-eight touchdowns and accumulated an impressive 93.8 passer rating. In 2009, he again compiled more than four thousand yards passing, becoming the first NFL quarterback to do so, and earned his first Pro Bowl selection. During the 2010 and 2011 seasons, Rodgers emerged as one of the premier quarterbacks in the league. In 2010, he guided the Packers to the team's fourth Super Bowl win and record thirteenth NFL championship, when they defeated the Pittsburgh Steelers, 31–25, in Super Bowl XLV; Rodgers was the game's most valuable player (MVP), passing for more than three hundred yards and three touchdowns.

In 2011, Rodgers earned his second Pro Bowl selection and was named to the Associated Press (AP) All-Pro First Team for the first time of his career, after becoming the first quarterback in league history to throw forty-five-plus touchdowns with six or fewer interceptions in a season. Rodgers helped the Packers record a league-best 15–1 record, and at the end of that season he was voted the AP NFL MVP and AP Male Athlete of the Year.

Known for his uncanny accuracy, superior arm strength, and cerebral approach to the game, Rodgers has refused to let outside influences disrupt his performance on the field. He explained to Nickel, "I have expectations of myself that are normally greater than the ones put on me and our team. . . . I just always felt there was more for me than what people expected of me." Packers head coach Mike McCarthy told Jim Corbett for *USA Today* (20 Jan. 2011), "He's definitely the quarterback we all hoped he would become. . . . He's definitely developed into a special player. He does it the right way. He's everything we hoped he'd be."

EARLY LIFE AND EDUCATION

The second of three sons, Aaron Charles Rodgers was born on December 2, 1983, in Chico, a city north of Sacramento, California. His older brother, Luke, is two years his senior, and his younger brother, Jordan, is five years his junior. Rodgers's father, Ed Jr., a chiropractor, met Rodgers's mother, Darla, a dancer who later became a homemaker, while attending California State University, Chico (better known as Chico State), where he was a standout offensive lineman for the school's football team. Rodgers developed a passion for football through his father, who had tried out unsuccessfully for several teams in the Canadian Football League before playing semiprofessional football with the Twin City Cougars of the California Football League for three-plus seasons, in 1978 and then from 1979 to 1981.

Rodgers began watching NFL games at the age of two, and by five, he was updating statistics of NFL players on his football cards and formulating game plans. Rodgers athletic abilities were apparent early on, and when he was a boy, he was reportedly able to throw a football through a tire strung from a tree. He grew up rooting for the closest NFL team, the San Francisco 49ers (the Oakland Raiders called Los Angeles home at the time), and idolizing the 49ers' legendary quarterback Joe Montana, who captured four Super Bowl titles in the 1980s. Rodgers admired Montana's ability to thrive in high-pressure situations and dreamed of following in his footsteps one day.

Rodgers was raised mostly in the Chico area, but he spent part of his elementary and middle school years in Beaverton, Oregon, where his father attended chiropractic school for three years. He has credited his father, who had worked a variety of jobs to support the family before settling on a career as a chiropractor in his late thirties, for instilling in him and his brothers a strong work ethic and sense of responsibility. "I'd see him go into the garage and study for four hours," he said of his father to Nickel. "I did not realize at the time, but he was doing it all for us." Because of his father's frequent job changes, Rodgers reportedly attended nine different schools growing up. He attended Vose Elementary and Whitford Middle Schools, in Beaverton, before moving back to Chico with his family in 1997. That year, he attended eighth grade at Champion Christian School, where, during the admittance interview, he boldly responded to a question about what he would do to make the school better by declaring that he would make their sports teams "really good," as his father noted to Karen Crouse for the *New York Times* (30 Jan. 2011). By that time, Rodgers had already excelled in youth-league football, basketball, and baseball, as a quarterback, point guard, and pitcher, respectively.

HIGH SCHOOL AND COLLEGE CAREER

Rodgers attended Pleasant Valley High School in Chico, where he played football, basketball, and baseball. As a sophomore, he made the junior varsity football squad. Despite his size (he was five feet six and weighed 120 pounds), Rodgers, who had large hands and feet, made an immediate impression on his coaches with his strong arm, sound mechanics, intellect, and football acumen. As the starting junior varsity quarterback for Pleasant Valley during his sophomore season, he called many of his own plays based on his ability to dissect and manipulate opposing teams' defensive schemes. One of his high school football coaches, Ron Souza, told Brad Townsend for the *Dallas Morning News* (1 Feb. 2011), "If he were to be tested, Aaron probably has a photographic memory. . . . Nine out of 10 of us are concrete learners. We have to learn motor movements by doing them over and over. Aaron could visualize what we wanted. You never had to doodle it up for him."

Rodgers made Pleasant Valley's varsity football team as a junior and, in his junior and senior seasons, passed for a combined 4,419 yards. He earned all-section accolades in both years (2000 and 2001) and set school records for touchdowns (six) and all-purpose yards (440) in a single game and passing yards (2,303) in a single season as a senior. Rodgers also pitched for Pleasant Valley's varsity baseball team as a senior; his fastball was reportedly clocked at 90 miles per hour. Along with his athletic achievements, he excelled academically, graduating with an A-minus grade point average and scoring a 1310 out of 1600 on his Scholastic Aptitude Test.

Despite a stellar high school football career, Rodgers did not receive any scholarship offers from NCAA Division I-A schools. Although he had helped Pleasant Valley's varsity team reach the sectional semifinals during both his junior and senior seasons, recruiters did not seriously recruit players from the school. Also, though he had almost grown to his adult height of six feet two, Rodgers had yet to fill out his frame, weighing under 200 pounds; he was deemed too small to play Division I-A football. As a result, he remained close to home and enrolled at Butte College, a junior college in Oroville, California.

Rodgers spent his freshman year at Butte and played on the school's football squad under head coach Craig Rigsbee, who lived in the same housing complex as his family. (Rigsbee literally walked over to Rodgers's home to offer him a scholarship to the school.) In his one season at Butte, Rodgers shined, throwing for 2,408 yards and twenty-eight touchdowns, with only four interceptions, and posting a completion percentage of 61.9. He also rushed for 294 yards and seven touchdowns. He led Butte to a 10–1 record, a NorCal Conference championship, and a number-two national ranking among community colleges. He was named both the NorCal Conference and region MVP and earned third-team all-America honors from JC Grid-Wire. Playing with a motley crew of castoffs, Rodgers recalled to Jarrett Bell for *USA Today* (7 Sep. 2008), "I was exposed to a ton of guys with different backgrounds and cultures. . . . Guys from Florida, Texas, and Canada. Guys at 25 and 26 years old, still trying to make it. My center was 25. Our free safety, the team leader, was 22 and had been to jail. To be, at a young age, able to get guys to play with you and raise their game, that was a huge lesson. Probably the best year of football for me, as far as personal development. I learned a lot about myself as a leader."

Because of his strong academic performance in high school, Rodgers was able to transfer to the University of California, Berkeley (Cal) after his freshman year. He was awarded a scholarship to play football by head coach Jeff Tedford, who had spotted him by accident while watching game film of his teammate, Butte tight end Garrett Cross. Rodgers, who had impressed Tedford with his arm strength and ability to read defenses, quickly learned Tedford's pass-oriented playbook and became the Golden Bear's starting quarterback in the fifth game of the 2003 season. He was soon named an offensive team captain and subsequently enjoyed one of the best seasons by a sophomore quarterback in the history of the Pacific-10 Conference (Pac-10, now the Pacific-12 Conference), passing for 2,903 yards and nineteen touchdowns, with only five interceptions, and amassing a completion percentage of 61.6 and 210 rushing yards. In his ten starts, he led Cal to a 7–3 record and helped Cal clinch its first bowl berth since 1996. In the 2003 Insight Bowl, Cal defeated Virginia Tech, 52–49. During the game, Rodgers threw for a collegiate-high 394 yards and compiled 424 yards of total offense, good for the third highest total in school history.

During his junior season at Cal, Rodgers again served as a team cocaptain and established himself as one of the best quarterbacks in American college football. He started in all twelve games and passed for 2,566 yards and twenty-four touchdowns, while posting a 66.1 percent completion percentage. He also had a passer rating of 154.4, which ranked second in the Pac-10 behind University of Southern California (USC) quarterback Matt Leinart.

Rodgers was selected as a quarterback for the All-Pac-10 First Team, finished ninth in the balloting for the Heisman Trophy as the top player in college football, and was named the Golden Bears' Co-Offensive MVP. In addition, he received all-America honors from the Associated Press and other organizations and earned Pac-10 All-Academic Second Team honors. Running an explosive offense that averaged more than thirty-seven points per game, Rodgers helped lead Cal to a 10–1 regular-season record (their only loss was to the USC Trojans, the eventual national champions), a number-four national ranking (the school's highest since 1952), and the 2004 Pac-10 championship. However, despite their record, the Golden Bears, lost out on a possible Bowl Championship Series berth to the University of Texas and were then upset by the Texas Tech Red Raiders, 45–31, in the 2004 Holiday Bowl.

Shortly after the disappointing bowl-game loss, Rodgers, who majored in American studies, decided to skip his senior season to make himself eligible for the NFL Draft. He finished his college career at Cal as the school's all-time leader in passer rating (150.3) and interception percentage (1.95). Speaking with Jason Wilde for the *Wisconsin State Journal* (7 Sep. 2008), Tedford described Rodgers as a "student of the game. He loves it. He submerges himself in it. He doesn't just memorize things. He understands concepts."

PROFESSIONAL CAREER

Analysts and scouts projected Rodgers as a top-ten pick in the 2005 NFL Draft, with some even considering him a potential number-one overall pick. However, the San Francisco 49ers, who had the top pick in that year's draft, passed on Rodgers after deeming him not "athletic enough," as Nickel noted. Instead, they selected quarterback Alex Smith of the University of Utah. Rodgers slipped to the twenty-fourth overall pick; the Packers believed he would eventually replace Favre. Despite being disappointed with his draft placement, Rodgers welcomed the opportunity to serve as an understudy to one of the greatest and most durable quarterbacks in NFL history. "I think the first progression every quarterback makes is you come in being the guy, and if you're not the starter you realize that there's someone better in front of you, and that's a big step to take because when you're the guy you're confident," he explained to Tom Silverstein for the Milwaukee *Journal Sentinel* (7 Sep. 2008). "Second, figure out the things he does that are better than you and study it and work on those things and improve." During the summer of 2005, Rodgers signed a five-year deal with the Packers worth $7.7 million.

BACKING UP FAVRE

During the 2005–07 seasons, Rodgers played only occasionally while serving as Favre's backup. During that time, he headed the Packers' scout-team offense in practice every day, where he was responsible for running upcoming opponents' offensive plays to prepare the defense. The Packers veteran wide receiver Donald Driver told Tim Layden for *Sports Illustrated* (7 Nov. 2011) that Rodgers "took every scout-team possession like it was the last possession of his life." While Favre made little effort to serve as a mentor to him during that time, avowing that it was not part of his job description, Rodgers made a point to shadow Favre as much as possible in practices and on game days in efforts to learn all the nuances of quarterbacking. "I'd watch him like a hawk," he noted to Silverstein, adding, "Anytime he opened his mouth in meetings to talk to a receiver I listened. . . . I wrote it down."

> *[Cal coach] Tedford described Rodgers as a "student of the game. He loves it. He submerges himself in it. He doesn't just memorize things. He understands concepts."*

In 2005, after performing poorly during the preseason, Rodgers made his NFL debut as quarterback for the Packers in a week-five matchup against the New Orleans Saints. Briefly replacing Favre in the fourth quarter of the game, which the Packers won 52–3, Rodgers completed his only pass attempt, to fullback Vonta Leach for no gain. That year, he played in two more games, in weeks fifteen and seventeen, against the Baltimore Ravens and Seattle Seahawks.

In the week-fifteen contest with the Ravens, in which the Packers lost handily, 48–3, Rodgers filled in for Favre near the end of the third quarter and completed eight of fifteen passes for sixty-five yards and one interception. In the game against the Seahawks, he entered for the game's final play in a 23–17 Packers victory. Despite winning the final game, the Packers ended the season with a disastrous 4–12 record, after entering the season having won three consecutive National Football Conference (NFC) North division titles. Packers head coach Mike Sherman, now the offensive coordinator for the Miami Dolphins, was consequently fired and replaced with McCarthy, who had spent the previous season as the offensive coordinator for the 49ers.

Rodgers developed further under McCarthy, a former quarterbacks coach, who required him to attend his mandatory quarterback school as part of the Packers' off-season program. During the school, which was held several days a week in six-hour sessions, Rodgers focused on improving his hand-eye coordination, his mechanics, and his physical conditioning. Despite his initial reluctance to make changes, Rodgers has said that the school helped him become a better all-around quarterback.

In 2006, Rodgers relieved Favre on two occasions (both times due to injury), appearing in games against the Philadelphia Eagles and the New England Patriots, in weeks four and eleven. In those games, he ran a total of thirty-six offensive plays, completing six of fifteen passes for forty-six yards, with no touchdowns or interceptions. After sustaining a broken left foot in the game against the Patriots, which the Packers lost 35–0, Rodgers did not play for the remainder of the 2006 season. The Packers improved their record from the previous year, going 8–8, but missed the playoffs for a second consecutive season.

Rodgers filled in for Favre on two more occasions during the 2007 season, in which he served as the Packers' primary backup quarterback for the third consecutive season. His duties included providing in-depth weekly reports to Favre and the team's coaches on upcoming opponents, which helped him gain superior knowledge of opposing teams' players and tendencies. During the season, Rodgers completed twenty of twenty-eight passes for 218 yards, throwing one touchdown. He had a passer rating of 106.0 and rushed seven times for twenty-nine yards. His first career touchdown pass came on an eleven-yard strike to wide receiver Greg Jennings in a week-thirteen game against the Dallas Cowboys. In that game, the Packers' rally, led by Rodgers, who completed eighteen of twenty-six passes for 201 yards, fell short, as the team lost to the Cowboys, 37–27.

Rodgers missed the final four weeks of the season because of a hamstring injury but returned to serve as Favre's backup during the postseason. The Packers finished the season with a conference-best 13–3 record and won their first NFC North division title since 2004. With home-field advantage throughout the playoffs, the Packers defeated the Seattle Seahawks in the NFC divisional playoff round, 42–20, the Packers played in the NFC Championship Game, losing to the eventual Super Bowl champions New York Giants, 23–20, in overtime. Rodgers played in the final series of the NFL divisional game against the Seahawks but did not play against the Giants in the NFC Championship Game.

RODGERS BECOMES THE PACKERS' STARTING QUARTERBACK

After Favre's long-delayed retirement before the 2008 season, Rodgers was named the Packers' starting quarterback. Although Favre abruptly unretired in training camp that year, the Packers ultimately settled on Rodgers as their quarterback; Favre was traded to the Jets. The decision to trade Favre, who had not only broken every major NFL passing record as a Packer but also appeared in a record 275 consecutive games (including the playoffs), greatly angered Packers fans, many of whom took out their frustration by heckling Rodgers in training-camp practices. Undaunted, Rodgers, who was also forced to deal with mass-media attention as a result of the Favre drama, handled the difficult situation—described by Silverstein as "arguably one of the hardest assignments in recent NFL history"—with poise and professionalism. McCarthy said of Rodgers to Wilde, "I think he grew up . . . I think he did a very good job of handling a challenge, handling a situation that there really wasn't a script for. It was unprecedented."

In his first season as a starter, Rodgers showed flashes of his potential to become an elite NFL quarterback. In his debut as a starter, in a game in which the Packers beat the Minnesota Vikings 24–19 on September 8, 2008, he completed eighteen of twenty-two passes, compiling 178 yards. Rodgers was the first quarterback other than Favre to start a Packers' game since 1992. The following week, he led the Packers to another victory, over the Detroit Lions, passing for more than three hundred yards for the first time in his career and throwing three touchdown passes; he was named the FedEx Air Player of the Week.

Rodgers suffered a partially separated shoulder early in the season but played through the injury, earning the respect of his teammates. He started in all sixteen regular-season games, passing for 4,038 yards and twenty-eight touchdowns with only thirteen interceptions. He became the fourth Packers quarterback to record four thousand or more passing yards in one season (after Favre, Don Majkowski, and Lynn Dickey) and only the second NFL quarterback to surpass the four-thousand-yard plateau in his first season as a starter (the first was Kurt Warner, who accomplished the feat as a member of the St. Louis Rams in 1999). Rodgers's numbers notwithstanding, the Packers finished with a losing 6–10 record and missed the playoffs. Seven of the losses were by seven points or fewer and included two overtime defeats. After signing a six-year, $65 million contract extension with the Packers in October 2008, Rodgers entered the 2009 off-season dedicated to improving his performance in come-from-behind situations.

ELITE STATUS AND THE PACKERS' RETURN TO THE SUPER BOWL

During the 2009 season, Rodgers became one of the top quarterbacks in the league. He started every game for the second consecutive year and threw for a then career-high 4,434 yards, thirty touchdowns, and only seven interceptions, while posting a remarkable 103.2 passer rating. He also rushed for 316 yards and five touchdowns. He was the first quarterback in NFL history to compile four-thousand-plus yards in each of his first two seasons as a starter and the first quarterback in league history with at least thirty touchdown passes, five rushing touchdowns, and seven or fewer interceptions in the same season. Early that season, Rodgers quickly put to rest any doubts about his ability to perform in high-pressure situations, when he led the Packers to a 21–15 opening-day, come-from-behind victory over the Chicago

Bears. In the game he threw a fifty-yard touchdown pass to wide receiver Jennings. Rodgers was the NFC Offensive Player of the Month in October, passing for 988 yards and posting a completion percentage of 74.5 and passer rating of more than 110 for the month. He earned his first career Pro Bowl selection during the season. The Packers finished second in the NFC North division, at 11–5, and advanced to the postseason. In a 51–46 overtime loss to the Arizona Cardinals, Rodgers threw for a franchise playoff best 423 yards and tied a franchise playoff mark with four touchdown passes.

Rodgers confirmed his status as an elite quarterback in 2010. Despite missing one regular-season game because of a concussion, he finished the year with 3,922 passing yards, twenty-eight touchdown passes, and a 101.2 passer rating, while adding a career-high 356 rushing yards and four rushing touchdowns. He was selected as a first alternate to the NFC Pro Bowl squad and was named the FedEx Air NFL Player of the Year. Despite losing fifteen players to injuries during the course of the season, the Packers finished second in the NFC North and earned the NFC's sixth playoff seed.

After winning road playoff games against the Eagles, the Atlanta Falcons, and the Bears, the Packers faced the Steelers in Super Bowl XLV, which was held at Cowboys Stadium in Arlington, Texas, on February 6, 2011. The Packers defeated the Steelers, 31–25, and Rodgers was Super Bowl MVP, completing twenty-four of thirty-nine passes for 304 yards and three touchdowns. Leading up to the Super Bowl, he posted one of the most dominating postseason performances in NFL history while setting several postseason passing records. In the NFC divisional round against the Falcons, Rodgers completed thirty-one of thirty-six passes for 366 yards and three touchdowns. His passer rating was 136.8, the highest in league postseason history among quarterbacks with at least thirty-five pass attempts. He also tied a league record in that game for throwing at least three touchdown passes in three consecutive playoff games.

Rodgers carried his dominant play from the 2010–11 playoffs into the 2011 regular season, posting the best numbers of his career. He finished the year with a career-high 4,643 passing yards, forty-five touchdown passes, and only six interceptions, and he amassed a league-best 122.4 passer rating, which is the highest single-season quarterback rating in NFL history. He became the first quarterback in league history to throw forty-five or more touchdown passes with six or fewer interceptions in a single season.

Rodgers was named to his second career Pro Bowl and first as a starter and earned his first AP All-Pro First Team selection. He also garnered NFC Offensive Player of the Month honors for September, October, and November and FedEx Air Player of the Week honors on six occasions. Bolstered by Rodgers's record-breaking numbers, the Packers won the first thirteen games of the season, finishing with a league-best 15–1 record. They won their first NFC North title since 2007 and earned home-field advantage throughout the playoffs, but they lost to the eventual champion New York Giants, 37–20, in the NFC divisional playoff round.

Despite the Packers' disappointing finish, Rodgers was recognized for his efforts during the regular season and won the 2011 AP NFL MVP award, receiving forty-eight first-place votes (second-place finisher, Drew Brees of the New Orleans Saints, received two). He was the first Packers player to win the award since Favre, who won three consecutive from 1995 to 1997, and the fifth Packer overall (after Bart Starr, Jim Taylor, Paul Hornung, and Favre). He was also named the 2011 AP Male Athlete of the Year.

PERSONAL LIFE

During the off-season, Rodgers, who is single, lives in Del Mar, an affluent beach town located twenty miles north of San Diego, California. In 2011, he signed an endorsement deal to be a spokesman for State Farm Insurance and has since appeared in a series of popular State Farm commercials for the company's "Discount Double Check" program, in which he pokes fun at his signature "championship belt" touchdown celebration. He has been involved in numerous charitable activities and worked extensively with the Midwest Athletes Against Childhood Cancer Fund. He is an avid fan of indie rock and country music and enjoys playing golf and the guitar in his spare time. He cofounded his own independent record label, Suspended Sunrise Recordings, which signed a Chico, California-based indie rock band called The Make.

SUGGESTED READING

Bell, Jarrett. "Leader of the Pack? Shadow of Favre Looms Large for Rodgers." *USA Today* 7 Sep. 2008: Sports 1C. Print.

Brown, Daniel. "Going Back to Mr. Rodgers' Neighborhood." *Mercury News* [San Jose] 5 Feb. 2011: News. Print.

Corbett, Jim. "Aaron Rodgers Is a Superstar QB out to Join Super Bowl Club." *USA Today* 20 Jan. 2011: Sports 1C. Print.

Crouse, Karen. "Packers' Rodgers Has Deep Roots in Chico." *New York Times*. New York Times, 30 Jan. 2011. Web. 6 Aug. 2012.

"Green Bay Packers: Aaron Rodgers." *Packers*. Green Bay Packers, 2012. Web. 6 Aug. 2012.

Layden, Tim. "All for One, One for All." *SI.com*. Time Warner. 7 Nov. 2011. Web. 6 Aug. 2012.

Nickel, Lori. "Does Rodgers Have What It Takes to Lift Team in Big Games?" *Journal Sentinel* [Milwaukee] 23 Oct. 2010. Web. 6 Aug. 2012.

Pells, Eddie. "Rodgers Fights Off Favre Legacy to Build His Own." Associated Press 5 Feb. 2011. Print.

Silverstein, Tom. "The Education of Aaron Rodgers: Young QB Has Had Plenty of Time to Watch and Learn." *Journal Sentinel* [Milwaukee] 7 Sep. 2008: S3. Print.

Townsend, Brad. "Patience, Perseverance Key for Packers Passer Aaron Rodgers." *Dallas Morning News*. Dallas Morning News, 1 Feb. 2011. Web. 6 Aug. 2012.

Wilde, Jason. "A Torch Passed: Aaron Rodgers Hopes to Make His Legendary Succession a Success." *Wisconsin State Journal* [Madison] 7 Sep. 2008: 3. Print.

—*Chris Cullen*

Janette Sadik-Khan

Born: 1960
Occupation: Commissioner of the New York City Department of Transportation

Janette Sadik-Khan is the polarizing, if prolific, commissioner of the New York City Department of Transportation (DOT). Taking her cues from cities abroad, Sadik-Khan's extensive reimagining of New York City's roadways have inspired other American cities to revamp their automobile-focused designs. What some call her almost self-righteous enthusiasm for bicycles and public space has won her fervent supporters and equally fervent detractors. "She's preparing us for a future that will have fewer cars," Sam Schwartz, a traffic consultant, columnist, and former traffic commissioner told Lisa Taddeo for *Esquire* magazine (Dec.

Bloomberg via Getty Images

2010). For a city of commuters, Sadik-Khan's vision of the future is difficult to fathom. Since 2007, when Sadik-Khan assumed her post, she has implemented more significant changes to the city's roadways than any of her predecessors since Robert Moses—the transportation czar who made New York City the paved paradise that it is today. Sadik-Khan disparages New York's labyrinth of bureaucratic red tape and her methods of reclaiming space for cyclists and pedestrians are often unusual. Ron Shiffman, a former commissioner of New York's Department of City Planning, told Dana Goldstein for the *American Prospect* (21 Nov. 2008) of Sadik-Khan: "She's a guerilla bureaucrat."

EARLY LIFE AND CAREER

Sadik-Khan was born in 1960 to parents Orhan Sadik-Khan and Jane McCarthy, who divorced when their daughter was seven. Her father was the late managing director of PaineWebber, an investment banking firm. McCarthy is an author and former journalist for the *New York Post* where she worked the city hall beat. She was also an environmental activist who worked with the Citizens Housing and Planning Council. Sadik-Khan grew up in the city, but traveled to California to attend Occidental College in Los Angeles. She graduated with a bachelor of arts in political science in 1982. She earned a law degree from Columbia University and became a member of the New York State bar. Sadik-Khan worked as a corporate lawyer before entering public service.

In 1990, Sadik-Khan joined the administration of New York City Mayor David Dinkins, a Democrat. She served as a senior advisor on mass transit. As a policy maker for DOT, she introduced several transportation initiatives that never came to fruition. In 1991, she suggested a toll at the East River bridges. The measure was inspired by a concept known as congestion pricing, in which motorists are charged for the use of heavily trafficked areas in an effort to tame gridlock. The project was shelved, as was Sadik-Khan's plan to install a light rail service, or above ground train, across Forty-Second street, amid objections from the Mass Transit Authority (MTA) and community groups. (She would reintroduce iterations of both projects under Mayor Michael Bloomberg.) During her tenure, Sadik-Khan was most famous for going after diplomats with unpaid parking tickets. When Dinkins lost his reelection bid to Republican Rudy Giuliani in 1993, Sadik-Khan moved to Washington, DC, where she worked for the Department of Transportation under President Bill Clinton. She worked on reforms to the bus manufacturing industry and developed an art-in-transit program before becoming deputy administrator at the Federal Transit Administration (FTA) where she managed the capital construction budget as well as federal assistance programs and policies.

In 1997, Sadik-Khan returned to the private sector as the senior vice president of the international engineering firm, Parsons Brinckerhoff. She travelled extensively with the firm, meeting with international transportation officials and generating ideas that would be fodder for her work in New York City. She was briefly considered for the position of commissioner of DOT in 2000 under Giuliani. She caught the attention of Bloomberg while consulting on the rebuilding of the World Trade Center in Manhattan.

TRANSPORTATION COMMISSIONER

In 2007, Bloomberg was considering two candidates for commissioner: Sadik-Khan and a man named Michael Horodniceanu, a former traffic commissioner in the Dinkins administration. Bloomberg was in his second term and looking to replace Iris Weinshall who was taking a teaching position at the City University of New York. Horodniceanu had ties to Weinshall, and was seen as the more "car-friendly" candidate, Annie Karni wrote for the (now defunct) *New York Sun* (14 Mar. 2007). Sadik-Khan on the other hand, made her interest in mass transit clear. Gene Russianoff, the chief attorney of the transport advocacy Straphangers Campaign, told Karni: "If the mayor is creative enough to pick someone like Janette, it sends a message that he wants to have a legacy in taming city traffic." Sadik-Khan was officially named transportation commissioner in April 2007.

Sadik-Khan oversees New York City's six thousand miles of street and twelve thousand miles of sidewalk, nontoll bridges, tunnels, and the Staten Island Ferry, which transports over sixty-five thousand commuters each day. While she does not control the city's sprawling system of subways, trains and buses, she often works in partnership with the MTA. As New York City's population continues to grow, the DOT has become concerned with issues of public and environmental health as well as traffic flow.

Although her changes have been implemented in a piecemeal fashion, Sadik-Khan is pleased with her progress. "There have been lots of things that have changed in New York City in the last 20 to 30 years. Our streets are not one of them," Sadik-Khan told Goldstein. "Our streets have really been designed as more utilitarian corridors to get cars as quickly as possible from point A to point B. Now there's a recognition that we can't keep doing that."

PLANYC AND CONGESTION PRICING

Sadik-Khan's appointment came the same month that Bloomberg unveiled a major sustainability agenda called PlaNYC. The 127 reforms on the agenda are based on reports that New York City will add one million people to its population by 2030. The goals of PlaNYC are to reduce New York City's carbon footprint by 30 percent, provide more public space and improve public health in a city where car exhaust permeates all breathable air. The blueprint—Sadik-Khan, in an interview with the European Cyclists Federation (14 June 2012) called the plan "a roadmap for managing the growth of the city"—was an abrupt departure from Bloomberg's earlier rhetoric concerning the future of the city; but his continuing support for Sadik-Khan has proven to critics that the administration is serious about sustainability. In 2008, Sadik-Khan introduced DOT's own "roadmap," a strategic plan called Sustainable Streets. Several of the policies outlined in the plan have been implemented, perhaps due to a lesson learned in Sadik-Khan's first year with DOT.

The original centerpiece of Bloomberg's PlaNYC was an effort to implement congestion pricing, charging cars eight dollars (twenty-one dollars for trucks) to travel below Sixtieth Street in Manhattan on weekdays. Sadik-Khan hoped to reduce the number of cars on the road—encouraging those who choose to drive within the city to use public transportation or a bicycle—and use the revenues to improve public transit. A majority of city dwellers supported the plan, as did the city hall, which approved the plan with a 30–20 vote in March 2008. The federal government promised the city $354 million to improve the mass transit system if the bill was approved by the state. Sadik-Khan and Bloomberg traveled to Albany to negotiate the plan, and adjusted it to appeal to suburb and outer borough citizens. Daily toll charges became tax deductible and the fee for taxis was dropped to one dollar. Still, state legislators in Albany crushed the initiative. They voiced their objections to Bloomberg's PlaNYC and Sadik-Khan, arguing that many of the initiatives benefitted people in the city at the expense of those in the suburbs. Assemblyman Jeffrey Dinowitz, as quoted by Michael Crowley for *New York Magazine* (17 May 2009), called Sadik-Khan an "anti-car extremist." Sadik-Khan's often brusque and some perceived, self-righteous, tone didn't win her any fans either. Queens City Council member John Liu told Crowley, "There is a sense of the elite telling the everyday people what's good for them, and that's simply not appreciated."

To her critics, Sadik-Khan argues that congestion pricing, an expansion of public space, and—perhaps her most divisive project—bicycle lanes aren't matters of elitism but of practicality. More than half of the city's residents do not own a car. As far as everyday people, she has told sources, the neediest New Yorkers rely almost entirely on public transportation while their health is seriously affected by car exhaust. And in response to anticar allegations, Sadik-Khan told Goldstein: "I'm radically pro-choice. I'm pro-all modes of transportation, not one mode elevated above all others, which I think has been the case in the past. We're really just trying to rebalance our system."

CYCLING ADVOCATE

Sadik-Khan seeks to improve the city from the perspective of cyclists and pedestrians as well as motorists and has looked to cities around the world for inspiration. She took a five-hour bike tour with the former mayor of Bogotá, Colombia. She visited Curitiba, Brazil, where they are making way for light rail through designated bus lanes. She has also traveled to Paris and London, where they successfully implemented congestion pricing in 2003. But one city in particular stood out to her for its innovative design. The city center of Copenhagen, Denmark—with its protected bike lanes, pedestrian promenades, and eighteen designated car-free areas—is a haven for cyclists and pedestrians. Sadik-Khan was so impressed that she hired Copenhagen's urban planner, seventy-two-year-old Jan Gehl, as a consultant in New York. (His fee was paid for with funds raised from private foundations.)

> *"There have been lots of things that have changed in New York City in the last 20 to 30 years. Our streets are not one of them."*

With the help of Gehl, Sadik-Khan implemented several designs similar to those in Copenhagen. In the Chelsea neighborhood of Manhattan, Gehl and Sadik-Khan erected what Sadik-Khan calls a "complete street," in which bike lanes are protected by a single lane of parked cars. Controversially, Sadik-Khan has turned over 250 miles of roadway to cyclists in the form of designated bike lanes. Though the number of cyclists in New York has increased, a majority of citizens do not own a bicycle.

Sadik-Khan has also painted hundreds of miles of bike lanes. Bike lanes have rapidly usurped auto lanes in the city, and some argue, without the input of the surrounding community. Businesses have complained that bike lanes and their surrounding buffers discourage motorists from pulling over to make quick purchases. Others, like Iris Weinshall who filed a lawsuit challenging a particular bike lane on Prospect Park West in Brooklyn, point to a larger issue. On his blog for the *New Yorker* website, John Cassidy wrote of the movement to create city bike lanes (8 Mar. 2011): "I support it. But the way it has been implemented . . . irks me to no end. I view the Bloomberg bike-lane policy as a classic case of regulatory capture by a small faddist minority intent on foisting its bipedalist views on a disinterested or actively reluctant populace."

Sadik-Khan insists that while she is committed to a sustainable future for the city, her greatest concern is safety. She argues that vehicle injuries are down 63 percent because of bike lanes and pedestrians plazas. Traffic fatalities in the city are at an all-time low. Sadik-Khan admits that her fervor to implement changes has made her unpopular in some circles, but Paul Steely White, the executive director of the advocacy group Transportation Alternatives, has defended her efficiency. "She takes her agency's mission of improving safety very, very seriously," he told Michael M. Grynbaum for the *New York Times* (4 Mar. 2011). "It's why she does things quickly, and it's why she does things sometimes too aggressively for people, but ultimately it's to save lives and to achieve a better balance on our streets."

Sadik-Khan is currently putting the finishing touches on a privately funded bike share program—another Copenhagen-inspired plan—in which people would pay a minimal fee to ride public bikes across the city. Stations for the bikes are planned throughout Manhattan and Brooklyn. It will be the largest bike sharing program in North America.

GUERRILLA BUREAUCRAT

As Manhattan real-estate prices indicate, space in New York City does not come cheap, and Sadik-Khan has bemoaned the lack of public space in the city for citizens to escape cramped apartments and for tourists to take refuge from the bustle. Working with Gehl, Sadik-Khan hopes to make the city friendlier to pedestrians. She launched a CityBench program, in which DOT installed a number of comfortable benches across the city to encourage walkers, and she's hoping to make the city easier to navigate with signage pointing the way to various neighborhoods and tourist destinations.

So far her most successful project, also designed with Gehl, has been a series of pedestrian plazas known as Broadway Boulevard. The creation of Broadway Boulevard involved the appropriation of two car lanes to create a public plaza in the middle of Times Square. The plaza features tables and chairs where people can gather and sit amid the billboards and traffic. White lines and barrier blocks made of recycled concrete separate the space. Similar plazas can be found along Broadway, which cuts through Manhattan's grid diagonally. Businesses surrounding the plazas—which are almost always full—report higher revenues, and help the city by storing the plaza furniture after hours in return. The success of Broadway Boulevard, has led to similar transformations in other places throughout the city including Madison Square and Herald Square. The plazas, like the bike lanes, appeared with surprising speed. One plaza in the Down Under the Manhattan Bridge Overpass (DUMBO) neighborhood of Brooklyn was created in one weekend. She told Taddeo that she made the space to send a message. "It was a quick way of showing you can transform a space in a matter of hours instead of a matter of years," she said.

Sadik-Khan has also instituted a program called Summer Streets. In its inaugural year, 2008, Sadik-Khan shut down Park Avenue for three Saturdays during the month of August. She opened the street to events like yoga classes and salsa dancing lessons.

As for mass transit, Sadik-Khan created a Select Bus Service, which operates like a bus rapid transit. The bus routes features designated bus lanes, new curbside fare collection and express stops. The service would greatly improve the city's reputation as one of the largest bus fleets in North America with some of the slowest routes. "I can't wish people onto a bus that's moving at two miles per hour," Sadik-Khan told Goldstein. "I have to give them service that encourages them to do it." Sadik-Khan hopes that bus lanes might encourage the city to move toward a light rail service. She points to Bogotá and Curitiba, two cities that are pursuing this tactic. She also hopes to create new ferry routes on the East River.

OTHER WORK

Sadik-Khan is president of the National Association of City Transportation Officials (NACTO), a coalition of transportation commissioners from thirteen major American cities; the group drafts national transportation policy and hopes to find direct federal funding for transportation projects for cities like New York, which must seek funding from the state's capitol in Albany. State representatives, most representing constituencies outside of the city, have been some of Sadik-Khan's most vocal critics. Sadik-Khan is also chair of the Transportation Research Board's Committee on Transportation Issues in Major US Cities and chair of the Reconnecting America board of directors, a national nonprofit organization. She is the founding president of a communications consulting company called Company 39. In 2011, Sadik-Khan won the Jane Jacobs Medal, named after the late urban activist who famously clashed with Robert Moses in the 1950s. In 2012, Sadik-Khan was selected as a David Rockefeller Fellow by the Rockefeller Foundation; the distinction encourages engagement between the public and private sector.

PERSONAL LIFE

Sadik-Khan met her husband Mark Geistfeld, now a law professor at New York University, while attending law school at Columbia University. The two married in 1990 and have one teenage son named Max. The family lives in New York City's West Village. Sadik-Khan often rides her bike—a Specialized Globe—to her office in the financial district.

SUGGESTED READING

Crowley, Michael. "Honk, Honk, Aaah." *New York Magazine*. New York Media, 17 May 2009. Web. 17 Aug. 2012.

Goldstein, Dana. "Street Fighter." *American Prospect*. American Prospect, 21 Nov. 2008. Web. 17 Aug. 2012.

Grynbaum, Michael M. "For City's Transportation Chief, Kudos and Criticism." *New York Times*. New York Times, 4 Mar. 2011. Web. 19 Aug. 2012.

"Janette Sadik-Khan: North America's Bicycle Super Star: Velo-city Talk." *European Cyclists Federation*. European Cyclists Federation, 14 Jun. 2012. Web. 17 Aug. 2012.

Karni, Annie. "Traffic Tsar Candidates Have Vastly Differing Visions." *New York Sun*. TWO SL, 14 Mar. 2007. Web. 17 Aug. 2012.

Taddeo, Lisa. "Janette Sadik-Khan: Urban Reengineer." *Esquire*. Hearst Communications, Dec. 2010. Web. 16 Aug. 2012.

—Molly Hagan

Sophie Theallet

Born: 1964
Occupation: Fashion designer

French-born designer Sophie Theallet became an overnight sensation in April 2009 when First Lady Michelle Obama wore one of her dresses to a public function. Theallet first honed her skills while serving as an assistant to Jean Paul Gaultier for five years before spending another decade as Azzedine Alaïa's right-hand woman. Since being catapulted into the international spotlight, she has launched her eponymous clothing line. Theallet credits her success to a simple formula: "I just try to make beautiful clothes done in a beautiful way," she said in an interview posted on the *New York Observer* website (11 Nov. 2008).

AFP/Getty Images

EARLY LIFE AND EDUCATION

The youngest of six children, Sophie Theallet was born in 1964 in Bagnères-de-Bigorre, a town in the southwest of France where she grew up with her parents and five older brothers. Theallet, whose father worked as a doctor, credits her family with instilling in her a love of fashion. "I have always wanted to be a fashion designer; I was almost predestined to be one by my history. My father's mother was a fashion illustrator and a very eccentric bourgeoisie woman in the thirties," she said in an interview posted on the *CIRCA Jewels* blog (14 Sep. 2011). "On my mother's side, they were industrials from the South of France and owned a factory that produced high-end wool blankets and dressing gowns."

Theallet was eight years old when she sketched her first collection. Her turning point came six years later, while visiting cousins in London. "[The trip] was a revelation. It was the peak of the punk movement, and I loved music. At the same time, Vivienne Westwood and Malcolm McLaren really inspired me with their strong fashions," she told Renée Schettler Ross for *France Magazine* (Summer 2010). Upon completing secondary school, Theallet decided to pursue fashion as a career. In 1982 the eighteen-year-old moved to Paris and attended Studio Berçot, a prestigious fashion design school.

APPRENTICESHIPS WITH GAULTIER AND ALAÏA

In 1984, after graduating a year early and winning the National Young Designer Award, Theallet was enlisted to create her own line of clothing for the Paris-based Printemps department store. Although her collection was a success, she decided against launching a fashion label and dedicated herself to learning her craft. She spent the next five years working for the renowned French couturier Jean-Paul Gaultier, whose avant-garde designs have since been worn by some of the world's biggest celebrities, including Madonna, Rihanna, and Beyoncé. During this period, she also worked with the fashion-forward Belgian designer Martin Margiela.

Theallet regarded her apprenticeship with Gaultier as a valuable learning experience. "I learnt from Gaultier to be fearless, to not be scared of your ideas and to have a unique voice," she recalled to Robert Cordero for the *National* (12 July 2009). "With him, I learnt my individual color palette and to create stories."

In 1989, Theallet served as the apprentice for another well-known designer: the Tunisian-born Azzedine Alaïa, dubbed the "King of Cling" for his body-hugging silhouettes. As Alaïa's right-hand woman, she regularly traveled with him and assisted him with his main collection, as well as his accessories and knitwear lines. He also helped enhance her cutting and draping talents. "Fit is very important, the way that clothes are done and cut, the woman has to feel the clothes," she explained to Hillary Latos in an interview for *Resident* magazine (Feb. 2012). "With Alaïa he made my eyes very sharp, and taught me how to do a fitting and defined what fashion is. It was the best experience you can have as a designer, if you want to learn, you learn from the best."

NEW YORK AND COLLABORATION WITH FRANÇOIS NARS

In 1999, a decade after she had started working for Alaïa, Theallet fell in love and moved from France to New York City. Over the next four years, she lived with her boyfriend at the Chelsea Hotel, a historic landmark in downtown Manhattan. Theallet served as a consultant, continuing to collaborate part time with Alaïa while also performing freelance work for other fashion designers, including Diane von Furstenburg and Rachel Roy. Theallet also created cosmetics bags, uniforms, and

T-shirts for Nars Cosmetics, a skincare and makeup line established by the celebrity makeup artist François Nars, who eventually sold his cosmetics empire in 2000.

In 2005 Theallet teamed up with Nars to establish Motu Tané, an exclusive, limited quantity line of upscale resort wear named after a French Polynesian island owned by Nars. The idea for the clothing line came from Nars, who was working on a book about Tahiti at the time. "I was really frustrated with the fact that I couldn't find any great fabrics to photograph," he told Marc Karimzadeh for *Women's Wear Daily* (28 June 2005). "I called Sophie and asked her if she could remake some vintage prints . . . and that's when we started talking about creating a collection and a lifestyle."

At the invitation of Nars, Theallet, who also held the title of chief creative officer for the collection, briefly took up residence on the main island of Bora Bora, which Motu Tané is next to, and which is renowned for the luxury resorts that overlook its famous turquoise lagoon. While there, Theallet conducted research on the original Polynesian textile designs for the line, which embodied a chic and jet-setting lifestyle. She also tried out different color combinations, dyed the original fabrics by hand in her kitchen, and incorporated a Polynesian patchwork method that is usually reserved for bed linens. "I try to mix the artisanal feeling of the island with what I learned in couture," she told Karimzadeh for *Women's Wear Daily*.

Launched in mid-October, the eighty-piece collection targeted upscale department stores and specialty boutiques, including Barneys New York and Jeffrey. The Motu Tané featured items made of lightweight and floaty fabrics, such as dresses made of Polynesian silk chiffon that contained details such as raffia halters and shell necklines; dresses with empire waists and gathered sleeves; crinkle chiffon blouses that were Victorian-inspired; and high-end printed T-shirts made of jersey. Other items in the collection included caftans, skirts, and bathing suits, as well as footwear and headgear. Following the launch, Theallet and Nars announced plans to make the line available year-round and to expand into fashion and home accessories.

SPRING 2009 COLLECTION

In 2007, after two years of collaborating with Nars, Theallet made the decision to launch her own collection with the help of her American-born husband, Steven Francoeur, who supervises production and sales. (The two met at a dinner party thrown at Alaïa's home.)

At that time, the couple's apartment, located in the New York neighborhood of Brooklyn Heights, served as Theallet's makeshift studio, while the kitchen table became the hub where Theallet performed her sketching and sewing, with the assistance of only one seamstress. Theallet would subsequently send the patterns that she had drawn for her clothing line to South Korea, Vietnam, and India, where they were printed on textiles and shipped back to her. From there, she would create a prototype of the garment, which she produced at a local factory. Theallet would then conduct a final appraisal of the item for quality control, wrapping, and labeling.

> **"I just try to make beautiful clothes done in a beautiful way."**

Theallet's clothing line made its runway debut in September 2008, at New York's Spring/Summer Fashion Week, which is considered the unofficial kickoff of the runway season. (It is among the four major fashion shows held in the fashion capitals of the world, including Paris, London, and Milan.) Theallet's ready-to-wear collection drew raves for her attention to feminine detail, which included pin tucks and draping. Cathy Horyn wrote for the *New York Times* (9 Sep. 2008), "The lines of her dresses—shirtwaists in boldly striped cotton, skimmy shifts in tropical prints or vivid orange silk with delicately pleated hems—were as modest as they were feminine."

Equally complementary was Laird Borrelli-Persson for *Style* (9 Sep. 2008), who wrote: "It's well-known that Theallet worked with Azzedine Alaïa for a decade before establishing Motu Tané, a resort line, with François Nars. But it was the influence of the makeup king . . . that was most notable in this extremely summery collection, which featured djellaba shapes, head scarves, crisp cottons circled with bright ribbon stripes, and tropical flowers appliquéd with satin."

Theallet also garnered headlines for her choice to cast only African American models. "I was thinking about colors, and they look amazing on dark skin, so it came naturally," she told Borrelli-Persson. She also said her decision paid homage to the legendary designer Yves Saint Laurent, who had recently passed away; the pioneering couturier was the first to have a show that exclusively featured black models.

RISING PROFILE IN FASHION CIRCLES

Theallet's fall/winter 2009 collection, which debuted in February 2009, drew inspiration from Native American styles. Similar to her spring collection, Theallet showcased a bold color palette and adorned her dresses with feminine details, including pleats, tiers, and pin tucks. Many of her outfits were accessorized with moccasin boots that were jointly designed with footwear manufacturer Sorel.

In April 2009 Theallet further raised her visibility in the fashion industry, when First Lady Michelle Obama donned one of her cotton shirtwaist dresses for a statue presentation ceremony at the US Capitol Visitor Center, in Washington, DC. In August of that year, Theallet was among ten emerging designers vying for the prestigious Council of Fashion Designers of America (CFDA) and Vogue Fashion Fund initiative, which provides the winners with a cash award and a yearlong mentorship from established fashion designers and executives.

A month later, Theallet unveiled her spring/summer 2010 line, which was a clear departure from her earlier collections. "Sophie Theallet is all fired up this season—showcasing, as she did, a collection that drew on a firey palette of oranges, burnt umber, ochre, peach and satiny saffron before moving onto striking color clashes; magenta and egg yolk yellow, egg yolk yellow and teal," according to Jessica Bumpus for *Vogue UK* (14 Sep. 2009). "Low-key and sparing use of print and pattern kept the collection to a safe wardrobe bet—as did wearable silky cami vests tucked into safari skirts, shirt dresses and the occasional frou frou number."

Theallet found herself back in the headlines in November 2009, when she was named recipient of the CFDA/*Vogue* Fashion Fund award. As the winner, Theallet received a cash award totaling two hundred thousand dollars; Oscar de la Renta also agreed to serve as her mentor. In February 2010, Theallet was one of twelve designers who were awarded affordable studio space in the Garment District from the CFDA Fashion Incubator program.

REMAINING A FORCE ON THE RUNWAY

With her winnings, Theallet expanded her fall/winter 2010 line to include knitwear. The ready-to-wear collection, which was also unveiled in February, embraced a bohemian style that revolved around fairy tale themes. "I was thinking about folklore and old children's stories that little girls grow up with around the world," she told *Interview* magazine (2010). "I want to bring back to women the lost memories and the magic we felt when we fell in love with our first princess dress."

Theallet's show, which was attended by renowned fashion editors such as Carine Roitfield and Suzy Menkes, also drew critical praise. "The show started with cozy knitwear but quickly morphed [into] hippy gypsy French floral dresses paired with tassled boots," Raakhee Mirchandani wrote for the *New York Post* (19 Feb. 2010). "The beauty is in the delicate nature of her fabrics, a smooth charmeuse, a sheer georgette and luxe velvets sell her message of bohemian beauty. And the standout piece was the soft pink pleated skirt paired with a red velvet off-the-shoulder top that solidified her place among the designers to watch."

Theallet's spring/summer 2011 line—a nod to Mexican culture—featured models in Frida Kahlo–inspired hairstyles sporting peasant blouses, tiered skirts, traditional lace, and bohemian printed sundresses. Strong women have influenced her subsequent collections. Female outlaw Bonnie Parker, of Bonnie and Clyde fame, served as the inspiration for Theallet's fall/winter 2011 collection, in which her models donned black berets, pencil skirts, printed and chiffon silk dresses, as well as wool coats and tailored suits. "Theallet's vision for winter was an ode to Parisian charm. The opening look, a black knee-length silk pencil skirt paired with a supple cerise deep V-neck blouse complete with beatnik black beret and choker, was a taste of the tough-chic masculine-feminine wares to follow," Indigo Clarke wrote for *Vogue UK* (15 Feb. 2011). "Menswear was also a reference point—a Forties-inspired oversized tailored trouser and suit jacket made an entrance along with a double-breasted silk overcoat, and boxy men's-style overcoat cropped and paired with a gossamer slip of a skirt."

In February 2011, Theallet teamed up with Nine West to launch a line of accessories, including shoes, handbags, and jewelry. Four months later she launched a resort collection that was inspired by the writer F. Scott Fitzgerald's wife, Zelda. Theallet's spring/summer 2012 line made its debut in September 2011 and was influenced by the classic 1969 French film *La Piscine*, a sexy psychological thriller. In her next collection (fall/winter 2012), Theallet presented vintage-inspired clothing, including floor-length gowns, wrap dresses, and slit skirts in a color palette that included red, burgundy, and fuchsia. The dragonfly served as the inspiration for her most recent ready-to-wear collection (spring/summer 2013).

In addition to her own collection, Theallet has also designed uniforms for the employees at New York's Gramercy Park Hotel. Theallet, a recipient of the International

Woolmark Award in July 2012, also has plans to expand her company in the future. "I want to make a lifestyle brand, just everything a woman needs," she told Tracey Lomrantz for *Glamour* (1 Feb. 2010). "At Gaultier and Alaïa I learned the accessories, so you will definitely see those at some point, but I can't say when or how for now—it's too soon."

Theallet lives in New York City with Francoeur, with whom she has a son.

SUGGESTED READING

Borrelli-Persson, Laird. "Sophie Theallet: Review Spring 2009." *Style*. Fairchild Fashion Group, 9 Sep. 2008. Web. 14 Sep. 2012.

Bumpus, Jessica. "Sophie Theallet Spring/Summer 2010." *Vogue UK*. Condé Nast Digital, 14 Sep. 2009. Web. 14 Sep. 2012.

Clarke, Indigo. "Sophie Theallet Autumn/Winter 2011–12." *Vogue UK*. Condé Nast Digital, 15 Feb. 2011. Web. 14 Sep. 2012.

Cordero, Robert. "Every Stitch and Detail Has a Purpose." *The National*. Mubadala Development, 12 July 2009. Web. 14 Sep. 2012.

Horyn, Cathy. "Pledging Allegiance." *New York Times*. New York Times, 9 Sep. 2008. Web. 14 Sep. 2012.

Karimzadeh, Marc. "Motu Tané Offering Resort All Year Long." *Women's Wear Daily*. Fairchild Fashion Media, 28 June 2005. Web. 14 Sep. 2012.

Mirchandani, Raakhee. "Sophie Theallet Fashion Week Review." *New York Post*. NYP Holdings, 19 Feb. 2010. Web. 14 Sep. 2012.

"Sophie Theallet's Making All The Right Choices." *Interview*. Brant Publications, 2010. Web. 14 Sep. 2012.

"Très Tree-Lined Chic." *New York Observer*. New York Observer, 11 Nov. 2008. Web. 15 Sep. 2012.

—*Bertha Muteba*

Wes Welker

Born: May 1, 1981
Occupation: Football player with the New England Patriots

Many football coaches and players have called the New England Patriots' wide receiver Wes Welker, who stands a mere five feet nine inches and weighs 185 pounds, the toughest pound-for-pound player in the National Football League (NFL). Known for his elusive quickness, sure-handedness, and precise route-running skills, Welker has used his unique skill set to emerge as one of the best slot receivers in the league. Despite posting record-breaking numbers in high school and college, Welker was repeatedly overlooked by scouts because of his unimposing size and subsequently went undrafted in the 2004 NFL draft. He began his NFL career when he signed with

Getty Images

the San Diego Chargers as an undrafted rookie free agent but was released from the team after only one game, leading him to sign with the Miami Dolphins.

After spending three modestly successful seasons with the Dolphins, Welker was traded to the New England Patriots. He has since established himself as a key member of a high-powered Patriots offense that consistently ranks among the best in the league, and he played a major role in securing the team American Football Conference (AFC) East Division titles in 2007, 2009, 2010, and 2011 and berths in Super Bowl XLII and Super Bowl XLVI. One of the NFL's most prolific receivers, Welker recorded at least one hundred receptions and one thousand yards receiving in four of his first five seasons with the Patriots. He has made four straight Pro Bowl teams (2008–11) and earned four Associated Press (AP) All-Pro selections (2007, 2008, 2009, and 2011) and has also set several franchise and league records.

EARLY LIFE AND EDUCATION

The younger of the two sons of Leland and Shelley Welker, Wesley Carter Welker was born on May 1, 1981, in Oklahoma City, Oklahoma. His father worked as an engineer for Southwestern Bell for nearly three decades; his mother worked as a nurse. Welker was drawn to sports through the influence of his brother, Lee, who is four years older. The two boys loved to play soccer and football and spent countless hours playing in the family backyard. Their parents signed them up for youth-league soccer teams in an attempt to delay their entry into organized football and other dangerous sports.

Welker's athletic talents were evident from an early age. Intuitive, strong willed, and extremely competitive, he developed a knack for scoring goals in soccer, and on one occasion, according to his father, he scored an astonishing seventeen goals in a single game. Like his brother, Welker attended Heritage Hall School in Oklahoma City, a small, independent, private school that educates children from kindergarten through high school. He started playing football in sixth grade after the school's coaches invited him to join the team based on his speed, which he had showcased while running sprints alongside some of his football friends during a practice. Welker came to the attention of Heritage Hall's varsity football coaches the following year, when his coach, Craig Brown, declared that Welker would become the best athlete in the school's history.

HIGH SCHOOL CAREER

Brown's bold declaration proved true as Welker emerged as an all-around star on Heritage Hall's varsity football squad. Under head coach Rod Warner, he became a standout on offense, defense, and special teams, as a running back, defensive back, placekicker, and punt returner, respectively. Despite his relatively small size, Welker became known for his hard-nosed and unrelenting style of play. Warner recalled to Jim McCabe for the *Boston Globe* (3 Dec. 2007), "He was a machine. . . . He would go at it so hard, all the time. He would not only kick off, he would be the first downfield to make the tackle. He would make a sixty- or seventy-yard play, handle the extra-point try, tilt his facemask back to throw up, then go out and kick off. He just never quit. I mean, never."

Welker's dogged versatility was put on full display during his junior season, when he rushed for 1,228 yards, made sixty-two receptions, and scored thirty-seven touchdowns while adding ten interceptions and eight field goals. That year he teamed up with his best friend, quarterback and future country music star Graham Colton, to lead Heritage Hall to a perfect 15–0 record and a Class 2A state title with a thrilling 35–34 victory over the Tishomingo Indians. In the state title game, Welker accumulated over two hundred all-purpose yards (rushing, receiving, and returning), scored three touchdowns, and recorded one interception. In another remarkable game, he scored ten points in the final thirteen seconds—scoring a touchdown, converting the extra point, booting an onside kick, and kicking a field goal—to lead Heritage Hall to a come-from-behind victory.

During his senior season, Welker led Heritage Hall to a 12–1 record and was named Oklahoma Player of the Year by the *Daily Oklahoman* and *USA Today*. He finished his high school career at Heritage Hall having accumulated 8,231 all-purpose yards. He scored a combined ninety touchdowns along with nearly two hundred tackles, twenty-two interceptions, and nine fumble recoveries.

COLLEGE CAREER

Despite his extraordinary accomplishments in high school, Welker was considered by college scouts to be too small and too slow to play National Collegiate Athletic Association (NCAA) Division I-A football (later renamed Division I Football Bowl Subdivision), the highest level of college football. Also working against him was the fact that he had competed in Oklahoma's Class 2A division, the second lowest of the six high-school athletic levels in the state, which prompted doubts about how he would fare against stiffer competition. Consequently, Welker received no scholarship offers from Division I-A schools.

In an effort to secure Welker a scholarship, Warner sent out more than one hundred DVDs of Welker's high school highlights to football coaches throughout the United States. One of those coaches was Texas Tech University's Mike Leach, who was intrigued by Welker's unique combination of skills. "When you saw him, he was slow and not really big," Leach explained to Jarrett Bell for *USA Today* (29 Jan. 2008), "but he just had a great sense of the field and how to play football." After another recruit opted to attend Boston College instead of Texas Tech, Leach offered Welker the university's last remaining football scholarship, which he immediately accepted.

As a freshman Welker joined the Texas Tech Red Raiders' starting lineup as a slot receiver and punt returner, roles he retained over the next four years. He thrived in Leach's pass-oriented offensive system and emerged as one of the most accomplished athletes in Texas Tech history, with coaches and teammates nicknaming him "the Natural." During his college career, he appeared in a total of fifty games and finished as Texas Tech's all-time leader in receptions (259) and receiving yards (3,069) while also setting NCAA career records for punt return yards (1,761) and punt return touchdowns (eight). Welker received the Mosi Tatupu Award for being the best special teams player in college football in 2003 and was selected to the All-Big 12 Conference First-Team in 2000, 2002, and 2003. Welker graduated from Texas Tech with a degree in management.

PROFESSIONAL CAREER

Welker's record-breaking college numbers notwithstanding, professional scouts once again labeled him too small and too slow to play in the NFL, and he was passed over by every team in the 2004 NFL Draft. He eventually secured a spot on an NFL roster after signing with the San Diego Chargers as an undrafted rookie free agent. "I knew I had a chance to at least see what I could do," he explained to Monique Walker for the *Boston Globe* (2 Oct. 2011). "I

> *"The one thing that separates [Welker] from other folks is his quickness and change of direction. He knows one speed and that's one hundred miles per hour."*

didn't know if I'd make the team or what would happen or anything like that leading up to the day before cuts. I had a good preseason. I didn't know what was going on." Welker made his professional debut on September 12, 2004, in the Chargers' season opener against the Houston Texans. In the game, which the Chargers won, 27–20, he returned four kickoffs for 102 yards. However, Welker was released from the team days later to clear roster space for safety Clinton Hart.

Soon after his release from the Chargers, Welker was signed by the Miami Dolphins. In fourteen games during his rookie season with the Dolphins, he returned fifty-seven kicks for 1,313 yards (an average of 23 yards per return) and scored his first career kickoff return touchdown on a 95-yard return in a game against the Baltimore Ravens. He also fielded forty-three punts for 464 yards, with an average of 10.8 yards per return. That season, Welker made NFL history in a matchup against the New England Patriots, during which he served as an emergency replacement for injured kicker Olindo Mare and became the first player ever to kickoff, make a tackle, kick a field goal, kick an extra point, and return a kickoff and a punt in the same game. He was subsequently named the AFC Special Teams Player of the Week for accomplishing the feat.

During the 2005 season, Welker served as a kickoff and punt return specialist for the Dolphins and also emerged as a wide receiver. That year he recorded twenty-nine receptions, sixty-one kickoff returns, and forty-three punt returns. Despite rumors that he would be cut from the Dolphins, Welker played in all sixteen games during the 2006 season, scoring his first career touchdown reception in a game against the Chicago Bears. Welker finished the season as the Dolphins' all-time leader in kickoff returns (166), kickoff return yards (3,756), and combined kickoff and punt return yards (4,988). The Dolphins, however, missed out on the playoffs for a fifth straight year after finishing last in the AFC East Division, with a record of 6–10.

NEW ENGLAND PATRIOTS

During the 2007 off-season, the Dolphins traded Welker, who had become a restricted free agent, to the New England Patriots for second- and seventh-round draft picks. The Patriots signed him to a five-year, $18.1 million contract. Impressed with Welker's elusiveness as a returner and receiver, Patriots head coach Bill Belichick recalled to Paul Tenorio for the *Washington Post* (29 Jan. 2008), "He killed us just about every time we played him. The only way we could really handle him was to double-team him." In his first season with the Patriots, Welker enjoyed a breakthrough year, starting thirteen of sixteen games and shattering career highs in every statistical category. Serving as the team's slot receiver, he set the Patriots' single-season record for receptions with 112, tying the Cincinnati Bengals' T. J. Houshmandzadeh for most in the NFL and breaking the record for most receptions by a player in his first season with a new team.

Along with fellow wide receivers Randy Moss and Donté Stallworth, both of whom also signed with the Patriots in 2007, and perennial All-Pro quarterback Tom Brady, Welker was part of an explosive Patriots offense that broke numerous NFL records, including most touchdowns in a season (seventy-five). The Patriots won a franchise-record fifth consecutive AFC East Division title and became the first team in league history to finish with a record of 16–0 during the regular season. The team won its first two playoff games, against the Jacksonville Jaguars and San Diego Chargers, respectively, and advanced to Super Bowl XLII. During the game, Welker tied the Super Bowl record for most receptions with eleven catches. The Patriots lost to the New York Giants, 17–14; nevertheless, the season was a significant one for the team, which became the first ever to win eighteen consecutive games in one season and the third team in league history to finish the year with a record of 18–1.

At the end of the season, Welker was named to his first AP All-Pro Second Team and received the Patriots' 12th Player Award for his invaluable contributions to the team. Describing Welker as a "tough, hard-nosed football player," Brady explained to Walker, "Different guys create different separation different ways. Wes uses his quickness a lot of the time and you see he gets a lot of separation because he is so good in and out of his breaks." Nick Caserio, the Patriots' director of player personnel, told Ian R. Rapoport for the *Boston Herald* (23 Dec. 2009) about Welker, "As a receiver, you have basically two jobs: to get open and catch the football. The one thing that separates him from other folks is his quickness and change of direction. He knows one speed and that's one hundred miles per hour."

Welker duplicated his success in 2008, when he led the Patriots in receptions (111) and receiving yards (1,165). He caught six or more passes per game during the Patriots' first eleven games, making him the first player in league history to accomplish that feat. Welker subsequently was named the Patriots' MVP for the 2008 season by *USA Today* and earned his first career Pro Bowl selection as a reserve for the AFC squad. He was also named to the AP All-Pro Second Team for the second consecutive year. The Patriots finished second in the AFC East with an 11–5 record after losing the division crown to the Dolphins in a tiebreaker.

INJURIES

During the 2009 season, Welker firmly established himself as a slot receiver, leading the league and setting a Patriots franchise record with a career-high 123 receptions and becoming only the fourth receiver in NFL history to record one hundred or more receptions in three consecutive seasons. He tied Herman Moore, who had caught the same number of passes for the Detroit Lions in 1995, for the second-highest reception total in league history. Welker also caught ten or more passes per game in seven games, matching the record Andre Johnson set with the Houston Texans in 2008, and ranked first in the AFC and second in the NFL with a 12.5 yards-per-return average (twenty-seven punt returns for 338 yards). Welker put up impressive numbers despite missing the second and third weeks of the season due to a knee injury and most of the regular-season finale against the Houston Texans after tearing two ligaments in his left knee early in the game. He earned his second Pro Bowl selection and was named to the AP All-Pro First Team for the first time in his career. The Patriots won the AFC East Division with a record of 10–6 and returned to the playoffs but were defeated by the Baltimore Ravens in the wild card round, 33–14. Welker did not play in the game due to his injury, which required off-season surgery.

Because of the severity of his knee injury, many analysts predicted Welker would miss most, if not all, of the 2010 NFL season. Nonetheless, after months of intense rehabilitation, Welker returned to the field to play in the Patriots' season opener. He appeared in fifteen of sixteen regular-season games and led the Patriots in receptions (eighty-six) while finishing second on the team in touchdown receptions (seven). He earned his third selection to the Pro Bowl, serving as a replacement for Johnson, who had been injured. The Patriots ended the season with a 14–2 record but lost to the New York Jets in the AFC Divisional playoff round, 28–21.

2011 SEASON

Welker had arguably the best season of his career to date in 2011, leading the NFL in receptions (122) for the third time and leading the AFC in receiving yards (1,569) and receiving yards per game (98.1), both of which were career highs. He also tied the NFL record for longest touchdown reception, catching a ninety-nine-yard touchdown pass in the season opener against the Miami Dolphins. He was named to his fourth consecutive Pro Bowl, earned his second Associated Press First-Team All-Pro selection, and helped the Patriots return to the Super Bowl for the second time in five seasons. Welker recorded seven receptions for sixty yards during Super Bowl XLVI; however, the Patriots again lost to the Giants, 21–17. During the 2012 off-season, Welker signed a one-year franchise tender with the Patriots worth $9.5 million.

PERSONAL LIFE

On June 24, 2012, Welker married his longtime girlfriend, Anna Burns, in a ceremony in Aspen, Colorado. The couple resides in the Boston area. Welker has established the Wes Welker Foundation (originally the 83 Foundation) to help assist at-risk youths in Oklahoma City. In 2010, he was recognized with the Ed Block Courage Award, an award named for the respected humanitarian and longtime trainer of the Baltimore Colts and awarded to one player from each NFL team each year for demonstrating exceptional sportsmanship on and off the field.

SUGGESTED READING

Bell, Jarrett. "Welker's View Improves: Patriots Receiver Moves from Sideline Festivity to Center of Super Bowl." *USA Today* 29 Jan. 2008: 1C. Print.

Bishop, Greg. "A Small Patriots Receiver Ends Up Being the Biggest Target of All." *New York Times* 4 Feb. 2008: D3. Print.

Carlson, Jenni. "Working Together: Wes Welker's Family Recalls Hard Work, Heartache and What It Took for Him to Reach the Top." *Oklahoman* [Oklahoma City] 27 Jan. 2008: 1A. Print.

Evans, Murray. "Back in Oklahoma, Story of Welker's Rise to Glory is Often Told." *Associated Press.* Associated Press, 2 Feb. 2008. Web. 16 July 2012.

Grossfeld, Stan. "Passion is in Fashion: Boston Has Four of the League Leaders in Intensity, and They Wear it Well." *Boston Globe* 24 June 2011, Sports sec.: 1. Print.

McCabe, Jim. "Yes Welker: Patriot's Refusal to Take No for Answer Got Him Where He is Today." *Boston Globe* 3 Dec. 2007: D1. Print.

Rapoport, Ian R. "Little Engine That Does: Pats' Welker Defies Odds as One of NFL's Best." *Boston Herald* 23 Dec. 2009: 64. Print.

Tenorio, Paul. "Young Receivers Are Rooting for the Little Guy: Pats' Welker Is a Big Influence." *Washington Post* 29 Jan. 2008: E4. Print.

—*Chris Cullen*